THE GOSPEL IN PICTURES

COMMUNICATING ETERNAL TRUTH VISUALLY

SCHOOL OF evangelism

DR. DANIEL KING

The Gospel in Pictures: Communicating Eternal Truth Visually

Published by: King Ministries Publishing
PO Box 701113 Tulsa, OK 74170-1113 USA
Website: www.kingministries.com
E-Mail: daniel@kingministries.com
Phone: 1-877-431-4276

ISBN: 978-1-931810-38-8

TABLE OF CONTENTS

INTRODUCTION

I'm a writer, so I spend a lot of time in coffee shops. I'm also an evangelist, so I look for ways to tell people about Jesus. What I've found is that the hardest part about witnessing is starting a conversation.

One day, I was reading a bibliography about Steve Jobs, the man who started Apple, the computer company. On the back of their Macintosh laptops, there is a picture of an apple with a bite taken out of it. I read that Jobs meant for the bitten apple to represent "forbidden knowledge." The allusion to the story of Adam and Eve in the garden of Eden is obvious. One day, I was looking at that apple and thought, "Why can't I use the Apple logo as a witnessing tool?"

So, I asked a friend to draw me a picture of a tree with Adam and Eve and a picture of three crosses so that I could use my laptop to witness to people.

Now, when I sit in a coffee shop to write, many people tend to stop and look at the back of my laptop. It gives me the perfect opportunity to ask, "Do you know what the picture means?" Then I share the Gospel. I have been able to lead many people to Jesus because of the sticker on the back of my laptop. One time I was on an airplane and a Muslim imam sat in the seat next to me. He asked me about the picture, and I had the opportunity to talk to him about Jesus for three hours because of the picture on my laptop.

After seeing the success of the picture on the back of my laptop, I realized that I also need a witnessing tool on my cell phone. I found a simple presentation of the Gospel online called "Three Circles." I made stickers with the Three Circles Gospel presentation and stuck them to the back of my phone:

Now, I have been able to use my phone to present the Gospel to many people. I carry my phone in my pocket everywhere I go, so by putting a witnessing tool on the back of the phone, it is always there if I need it. Plus, having a reminder on my phone reminds me to be a witness every time I pull my phone out.

The use of these two pictures in witnessing showed me the power of using a visual image to creatively share with someone about Jesus. I started looking for other images that can be used to talk about salvation. I found "The Bridge," "the Chair," "the Gospel Icon," "the Romans Road," and a variety of other images that you will learn about in this book.

In Acts 16:30, a jailer asked Paul and Silas the question that every evangelist loves to hear, "What must I do to be saved?" If you were sitting in a coffee shop and someone asked you this question, would you be prepared to answer it? After you read this book, you will be able to grab a napkin and a pen and sketch out a simple plan of salvation.

As an evangelist, I travel to many different nations. I have found that these images can even be used cross-culturally. Some of the countries that I visit have low rates of literacy. In these nations, a picture is a helpful way to communicate with people who do not know how to read. Pictures are universal. The meaning of symbols can be recognized in almost every culture and language on earth. Pictures are also an effective way to teach children how to understand and remember the plan of salvation.

Pictures are not a new way of communicating the Gospel. If you visit a medieval Cathedral, you will probably see beautiful paintings or stained-glass windows that depict Bible stories. Upon closer examination, these paintings and windows are full of iconography that use images and symbols to communicate powerful Gospel truths.

Back when common peasants were mostly illiterate, pictures were used as a powerful teaching tool. Even though more people know how to read in modern times, pictures are still an effective way to communicate.

So, in this book, I offer you a variety of ways to visualize the core message of the Bible. These pictures can help you in several ways. First, each picture can be used to lead a sinner to Christ. Second, the pictures will help you to remember how to present the Gospel in a simple manner. The pictures will give you a visual outline to follow as you share the truth. Third, I pray that these different methods will give you the boldness to be a witness. Fourth, being familiar with these different ways of talking to people about Jesus will prepare you to speak to different people with different needs in different situations.

Some people are auditory learners, other people are visual learners. These pictures help believers remember how to share the Gospel and they help sinners understand the Gospel easily. In today's sight and sound generation, we can have a bigger impact by communicating through both the eyes and the ears.

For each picture, I share the key Scriptures used, the source of the method, a script that can be used with the picture, and some thoughts about the advantages and disadvantages of each method. I did not create most of these methods of presenting the Gospel, but I have seen these concepts used in many different tracts and videos. The reason that I wrote this book is to review these various witnessing methods. In each example, I endeavor to credit the person or organization who originally developed each idea. Some of the images I found have been around for a long time while others are relatively new. Regardless of where these ideas came from, each drawing is a valuable way of talking to people about Jesus.

However, I do want to offer one caution. Reinhard Bonnke recorded a powerful video about evangelism. It takes place on a big ship in the middle of the ocean. Inside the ship's dining room, the crew is debating about the proper method of rescuing people who are drowning in a storm. Suddenly, a violent storm arises. The ship receives a distress call from a small boat that is sinking. Instead of going to rescue the people in distress, the people in the dining room continue to debate the proper method to rescue people. Only one brave man goes and throws a lifeline to those who are drowning. The point of the video is clear. Often the church spends too much time debating about the proper way to lead someone to Christ and not enough time actually going out and leading people to Christ. God has not called the church to be a cruise ship, but a rescue boat.

In the same manner, this book is not meant to be a debate about the proper way of leading a lost person to Jesus. Instead, this book is meant to spark a passion for lost souls in your heart. I am not trying to entertain you or educate you, I am trying to provoke you. I want these pictures to be tools that you use to actually lead people to Jesus.

The truth is that any one of these methods can be used by the Holy Spirit to rescue a lost person from an eternity in hell. The method or script that you use is not important. What is important is that you do something to share the Gospel. As you open your mouth and begin to speak, the Holy Spirit will give you words to say that will help you lead the lost to Christ.

Experiment with these different pictures. Find one that you like. Get to know it inside and out. Memorize the verses that are used. Learn how to share the Gospel at the drop of a hat. Be ready at all times. Look for opportunities to talk about Jesus and I pray that you will be used to rescue many people from hell.

CHAPTER 1

THE BRIDGE

Key Scriptures: Proverbs 14:12, Romans 3:23, Isaiah 59:2, Ephesians 2:1, Romans 6:23, John 17:3, Acts 16:31, Ephesians 3:12, John 3:16-18, John 3:26.

Source: Bill Bright taught a version of The Bridge in his presentation on the "Four Spiritual Laws,"[1] the Navigators use this illustration in their presentation on the "Bridge to Life,"[2] and Sonlife also uses the bridge illustration in their tract on "Knowing God Personally."[3]

WHAT TO SAY:

One of the most important questions people ask is, "How can I know God?" Other people wonder, "How can I get to heaven?" Many people think that if they do enough good deeds or enough religious activities, they will be able to earn their way to heaven. But is that true?

The challenge with knowing God is that there is a great separation between sinful humanity and a holy God.

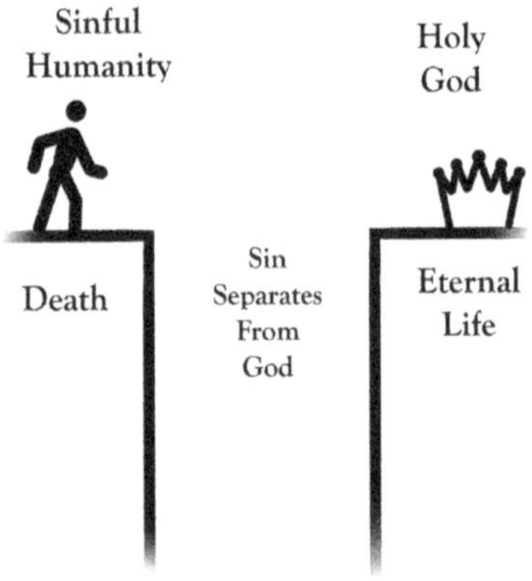

1 Bill Bright, "Would You Like to Know God Personally?" Accessed February 3, 2023, http://www.4laws.com/laws/englishkgp/default.htm

2 Navigators, "The Bridge to Life," Accessed February 3, 2023, https://www.navigators.org/resource/the-bridge-to-life/

3 Sonlife, "Know Him Personally," Accessed November 29, 2021, https://knowhimpersonally.com/

At the beginning of time, there was no separation between God and humans. God created the first humans, and He had a daily relationship with them. But then, because of sin, humankind was separated from God.

Now, God is in heaven and humans are here on earth. God is holy and all humans are sinful. What caused this separation? What messed up our relationship with God? The answer is sin.

What is sin? Sin is disobeying God's commands. God says, "Thou shalt not lie." Yet, people lie. God says, "Thou shalt not steal." Yet, people steal. According to Isaiah 59:2, this sin separates us from God: *"Your iniquities have separated you from your God; And your sins have hidden His face from you"* (NKJV).

Everyone has sinned. According to Romans 3:23, there is no one who is perfect, *"For all have sinned and fall short of the glory of God"* (NKJV). Sin separates us from God.

Because of sin, we are stuck here on earth living in a state of spiritual death. According to Ephesians 2:1, we are *"...dead in trespasses and sins."* According to Romans 6:23 there is a price that must be paid for our lives of sin: *"For the wages of sin is death..."*

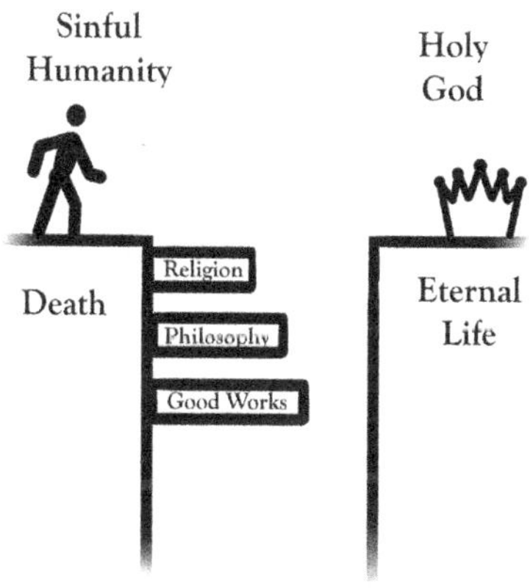

Inside every human, there is a desire to be connected with God. There is a God-shaped hole inside every one of us and we have an inner need to be reconnected with our Creator. There are a variety of ways that humans have tried to bridge the gap between heaven and earth. Some have tried religion, others have tried philosophy, and still, others have tried to reconnect with God through good works. Other people have tried to reach God through money, morality, or education.

None of these paths lead to God. The gap between heaven and earth is too large. It is impossible for us to bridge this gap through our own efforts. We all *"fall short"* (Romans 3:23) of the glory of God.

Even if we think that we are doing right, we cannot do enough to earn our way into heaven. *"There is a way that seems right to a man, but its end is the way of death"* (Proverbs 14:12 NKJV).

There is only one way for us to have eternal life or to reconnect with God. The Bible tells us that the only way for us to have peace with God is through Jesus Christ (Romans 5:1). According to John 17:3, *"...this is eternal life, that they may know You, the only true God, and Jesus Christ whom You have sent"* (NKJV).

This is the Gospel, the "good news" of Jesus Christ. God did not want humanity to be eternally separated from Himself. So, God provided a way for us to get to Him. According to John 3:16-18, *"For God so loved the world that He gave His only begotten Son, that whoever believes in Him should not perish but have everlasting life. For God did not send His Son into the world to condemn the world, but that the world through Him might be saved. "He who believes in Him is not condemned; but he who does not believe is condemned already, because he has not believed in the name of the only begotten Son of God"* (NKJV).

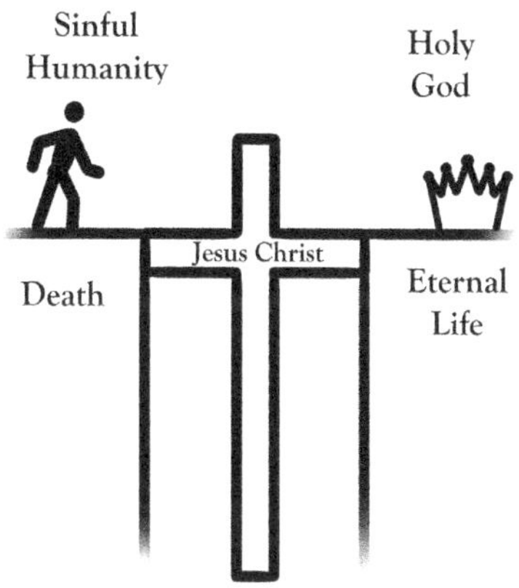

Jesus, the Son of God, came from heaven to earth. He died on a cross to pay the price for our sins. He did not deserve to die since He never sinned. Instead, He died as a sacrifice in our place. But He did not stay dead. After three days, Jesus rose from the dead and today He is still alive.

Romans 6:23 tells us that "*the gift of God is eternal life in Christ Jesus our Lord*" (NKJV) and Ephesians 2:1 tells us that we who were dead in sin are "*made alive*" through Jesus Christ. When Jesus died on the cross, He became the bridge between heaven and earth. Jesus is The Way who leads us from death to eternal life and from sin to salvation.

How do we cross over from death to life? In order to be saved from sin, we have to choose to believe in Jesus Christ. Acts 16:31 proclaims, *"Believe on the Lord Jesus Christ, and you will be saved, you and your household"* (Acts 16:31 NKJV).

It is through Jesus and His death on the cross that we gain the opportunity to cross over from a spiritual death to a living relationship with God. We do this through Jesus with "*...whom we have* *boldness and access with confidence through faith in Him"* (Ephesians 3:12 NKJV).

In order to know God, we have to call on Jesus for salvation. Acts 2:21 promises, *"Everyone who calls on the name of the Lord shall be saved."*

John 3:36 promises us that *"He who believes in the Son has everlasting life; and he who does not believe the Son shall not see life, but the wrath of God abides on him"* (NKJV). If you want to experience eternal life, then you can call out to Jesus right now for salvation. First, admit that you have sinned. Second, ask Jesus to forgive your sins and give you eternal life.

Your prayer could sound like this: "Dear Jesus, I know I am a sinner and I ask you to forgive me. I believe that you died on the cross so that my sins could be wiped away. I believe that you rose from the dead and today, I make you the Lord of my life. I choose to trust You and follow You. In Jesus' name, Amen." The exact words are not important, but what is important is whether your heart really means it.

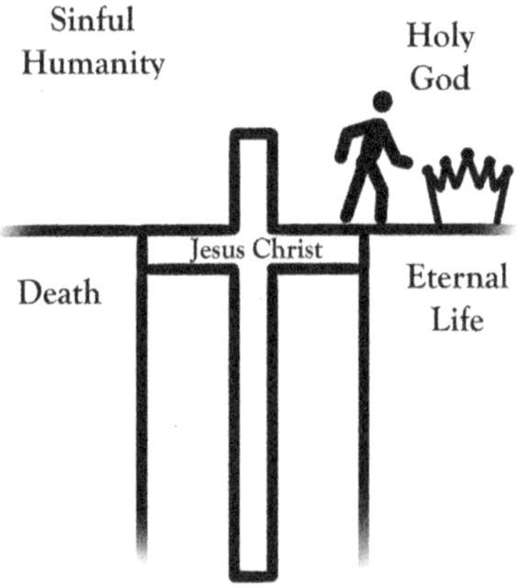

When you call on Jesus, you cross over from death to life. John 5:24 promises, "*...he who hears My word and believes in Him who sent Me has everlasting life, and shall not come into judgment, but has passed from death into life.*" Jesus is the bridge to heaven.

Thoughts About the Bridge

- I have seen different versions of the Bridge picture used in many different Gospel tracts.

- I like the picture of the Bridge because it clearly conveys the idea of passing over from death to life, from sin to forgiveness, and from earth to heaven. The gap between humanity and God provides the perfect opportunity to communicate the inability of humans to get to heaven through their own efforts.

- The Navigators[4] use the Bridge illustration in their One Verse Evangelism presentation using Romans 6:23. Here is how they emphasize each word from Romans 6:23 as they draw the picture of the bridge.

4 The Navigators, "One Verse Evangelism" (Accessed February 10, 2023), https://www.navigators.org/resource/one-verse-evangelism/

One Verse Evangelism

For the Wages of Sin is Death
But the Gift of God is Eternal Life
in Christ Jesus our Lord.
Romans 6:23

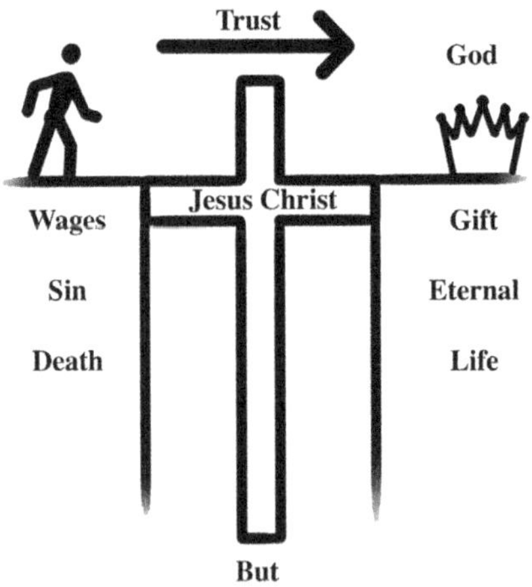

- I often preach a dramatic message at my mass crusades based on this illustration. Here is how I preach this message using actors to visually illustrate the message.

Characters: God the Father, Adam, Eve, Jesus

At the beginning of time, God created Adam and Eve. They were the first man and the first woman. *(I invite an older man to play the part of God and a young man and woman to play the parts of Adam and Eve).*

Every day, God would walk with them and talk with them. *(God takes Adam and Eve by the hand and walks around the platform with them.)*

But one day, Adam and Eve sinned. Sin is when we disobey God's commands. Lying, cheating, stealing, and having hate in our hearts is sin. *(Adam and Eve remove their hands from God's hand).*

Sin separated humankind from God. This is why God hates sin. Sin causes a large gap or chasm between God and human beings. *(Adam and Eve go to one side of the platform and God stands on the other side of the platform).*

For many centuries, humans have tried to cross this gap so that they could have a relationship with God.

Some people think, "If I study many books, I can figure out how to get to God." But no matter how much you study, you cannot learn how to cross the gap. *(Adam and Eve pretend to study books.)*

Other people think, "If I can make lots of money, I can buy my way into heaven." But no matter how much money you have, you can never purchase a way into heaven." *(Adam and Eve pretend to have money.)*

Still, others think, "If I become religious and do many religious rituals, I can restore my relationship with God." But the problem with religious rituals is that they are not enough to cross the enormous gap that exists between heaven and earth. *(Adam and Eve kneel down to pray.)*

God knows that it is impossible for humans to figure out a way to get to heaven, so He came up with a plan. He called His only Son, Jesus Christ, and told Him, "I want you to go to earth. You will be born as a baby to a virgin named Mary. You will become a man and I want you to make a way for humans to come to heaven." *(The man playing God the Father talks to Jesus and explains the plan to Him).*

So, Jesus, the Son of God, was born as a baby. He grew up and walked the dusty streets of Israel. He had twelve disciples and He walked with them and talked with them every day. He taught them about His Father in heaven. *(Jesus takes the hands of Adam and Eve and they become his disciples. He leads them around the platform and pretends to talk to them.)*

But some evil men crucified Jesus on a cross. He was innocent. Jesus did not deserve to die. People who sin deserve to die because the price for sin is death, but Jesus never sinned. *(Adam and Eve stretch out Jesus' hands and pretend to drive nails into His hands and feet.)*

Jesus died on the cross. He shed His blood so that our sins could be forgiven. But Jesus did not stay dead. After three days, Jesus rose from the dead and even today, Jesus is alive! *(Jesus comes back to life!)*

When Jesus died on the cross, He became the bridge between heaven and earth. Jesus said, "I am the way, the truth, and the life, no one comes to the Father except through me." *(Jesus stands in the middle of the platform and stretches out His hands.)*

Now, every person must make a choice to either accept Jesus Christ as Savior or reject Him. If you accept Jesus as your Savior, you will go to heaven when you die. If you reject Him, you will go to hell. If you make Jesus the Lord of your life, you can be reunited with God, but if you reject Him, you will be forever separated from God. Do you want to accept Jesus or reject Him? *(I ask the person playing Adam if he wants to accept Jesus. He says, "Yes!")*

If you want to choose to follow Jesus today, then repeat this prayer after me. "Dear God in Heaven, I believe Jesus died on the cross. I believe Jesus rose from the dead. I repent of my sin. Today I choose to follow Jesus for the rest of my life. Jesus, please forgive me. In

Jesus' name, Amen." *(I ask Adam to kneel down at the feet of Jesus and I lead him in the prayer.)*

When you pray to Jesus, He becomes your bridge to heaven. *(Jesus lifts Adam to his feet and introduces him to God the Father. God responds by hugging Adam and welcoming him to heaven.)*

Do you want to pray to Jesus? *(I ask Eve if she will also pray with me. She also repeats the prayer of salvation with me and is welcomed to heaven.)*

Today, God wants to walk with you and talk with you. If you want Jesus to become your bridge to heaven, lift your hand high. *(After the audience responds, I lead them all in a prayer of salvation).*

CHAPTER 2

THE CHAIR

Key Scriptures: *"As many as received Him, to them He gave the right to become children of God, even to those who believe in His name"* (John 1:12)

Is Your Life Self-Directed or Christ Directed?

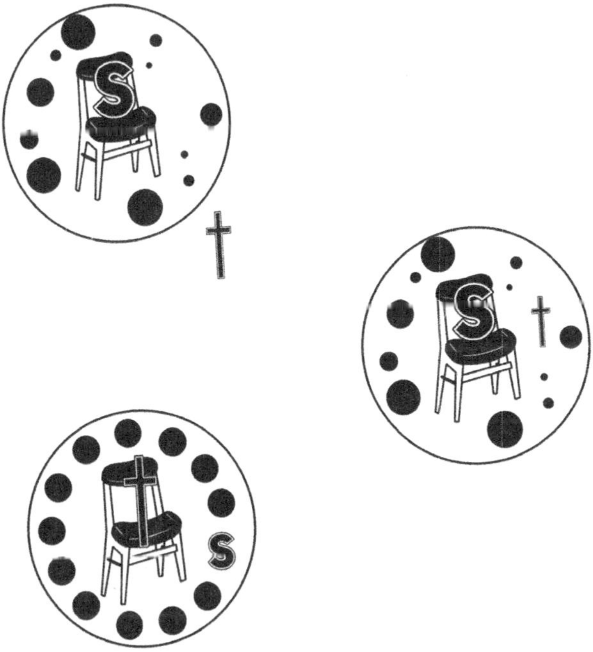

Source: Bill Bright in his presentation on the "Four Spiritual Laws[5]."

Key Question: Who is sitting on the throne of your heart?

WHAT TO SAY:

I will show you three pictures and I want you to tell me which one of these three pictures best depicts your life.

At the center of each picture is a chair. The chair represents the throne of your life. The throne of your life is where you make all of your decisions. This is where you decide how you behave, what your priorities are, who you will marry, and what your attitude will be like. All of the smaller circles represent your various goals and priorities.

In the first picture, the big "S" is sitting on the chair. The big "S" represents "Self." By putting yourself on the throne of your life you are saying, "I am in charge of my life. I make my decisions and I do what I want."

5 Bill Bright, "Would You Like to Know God Personally?", Accessed February 3, 2023, http://www.4laws.com/laws/englishkgp/default.htm

In this picture, you will notice the cross is outside the circle. The cross represents Jesus Christ. Living with Jesus outside of your life means that God has no place in your life. You make all your own decisions, and you couldn't care less about what God wants you to do.

In the second picture, the big "S" is still sitting on the throne of your life. You still make all of your own decisions, but now the cross (which represents Jesus) is inside of the circle of your life. If this circle depicts your life, it means you have allowed God to have a small place in your life. Someone whose life looks like this circle may go to church on Sunday or they may occasionally say a prayer, but God is only one small priority out of many priorities in their life.

In the third circle, you will notice the big "S" is no longer on the chair. Instead, the cross has been placed on the throne of this life. This signifies that you have given your life to Jesus Christ and decided to follow His plan for your life. Instead of making all your own decisions and doing things your way, you have decided to live your life in the way that God wants you to live your life. The person in this circle has placed Jesus in the pilot seat and they have moved over to the seat of the co-pilot. Notice that all of the circles are now the same size and are evenly distributed around the circle. This is because God helps us to put every other aspect of our lives in the proper order and the proper place.

Which of these three circles best represents your life? Perhaps you are like the first circle and God has no place in your life at all. Or perhaps you are like the second circle, and you think about God occasionally, but you have not fully surrendered your life to Him. Or perhaps you have decided to completely follow God's plan for your life.

Which of these three circles would best represent the state of your life right now?

Which circle would you like to represent your life?

Thoughts about The Chair

- The Chair illustration is a useful diagnostic question to determine where a person is in their walk with God. Some people have no place for God in their lives. Others have made a place for God in their lives, but have not made Him the center of their lives. The third type of person has placed Jesus in the center of his or her life and has decided to completely follow Him.

- When I preach this illustration in front of an audience, I combine the visual presentation with a little drama that also uses a chair. I invite a volunteer up from the audience and I ask her to sit down in a chair. Then I ask her to stand up. I have her sit down and stand up several times. Then I ask her to almost sit down. As she is half sitting, half standing, I ask the audience, "Is almost sitting the same as sitting?" Everyone replies, "No."

Then I read Acts 26:28, "Then Agrippa said to Paul, "You almost persuaded me to become a Christian." I ask, "Is almost becoming a Christian the same as becoming a Christian?"

If someone is almost sitting, they are not fully sitting, and if someone is almost a Christian, they are not a Christian. In order to become a Christian, we must fully commit to following Christ.

| CHAPTER 3 |

THE GOSPEL ICON

Key Scriptures: (God's Creation) Genesis 1:1, (Satan's Deception) Genesis 3:4-5, (Christ's Substitution) Romans 5:8, (Our Redemption) John 10:10

The Gospel Icon

Source: T.L. Osborn[6], Ladonna Osborn[7]

WHAT TO SAY:

When I approach people, I say, "Did you know that God loves you and that He has a plan for your life?" They tend to say, "Well, what plan?" I say, "Let me tell it to you this way."

God's Creation

In the beginning, God had a plan. We call creation God's creation because He created everything, and in that plan, we see that He created with a purpose. He had a purpose for everything He created.

According to the Bible, which we understand is the word of God that reveals God's good plan to us, it tells us that everything that He created was for humankind since God made people, you and me, in His own image.

6 "Osborn Ministries International", Accessed February 3, 2023, https://osborn.org/about/osborn-ministries-international

7 Ladonna Osborn, personal interview, May 18, 2018.

Did you know that God made you in His image? You've never known that? You don't feel like you've been made in God's image, but that's the truth, and God's brought me across your path to tell you things that He wants you to know, so think about this.

God's creation, in the beginning, was perfect. Everything functioned beautifully because God and his creations, Adam and Eve, walked in harmony. Everything worked right. There was no sickness. There was no poverty. There was no anger. There was no insecurity. There was no injustice. There was nothing that was contrary to God's good plan. Everything that was good came through God, and so, when God made everything, He made it perfect. He made you, and in the beginning, humanity was perfect. But then the question comes: "Well, I look around my world; I look at my life, my family, how I feel, the troubles that I have, and so what? Did God cause this? What happened? Where did it go wrong?"

Satan's Deception

Well, the story continues in the Bible, and we learn about what we call Satan's deception. Satan is the enemy of God, and, according to the Bible, he came into the garden that God had created for Adam and Eve, God's first human creations, and he deceived them. He questioned whether God's word was true.

Satan said, categorically, "God did not say that," and, "It will not happen the way God said." You see, Satan is a liar, and he lied to Adam and Eve, but they believed him rather than believing what God had told them. God created them for relationship, but look at what happened. The enemy of God came in and deceived them.

Here's something to think about. God had created, within humankind, the power to make a choice. I don't know why He did that because Adam and Eve used that choice power to choose the lie rather than the truth, to choose the enemy of God rather than their loving Heavenly Father, the Creator. Yet when they chose to believe the lie, here's what happened. Satan caused them to question God's integrity. You see, the relationship between God and people was held together by trust. They didn't have to trust God. They didn't have to obey God. They didn't have to respond to his love. They had a choice. I don't know why He did that because, when they made the choice, look at what happened. They were entrapped by the very one who had promised them everything because he's a liar, but at the moment that they doubted God, the trust was broken and something terrible happened. The relationship that they had enjoyed with God was broken. God didn't want that, but when it was broken, all that had gone on in them that was perfect, fulfilling, and purposeful, and God's plan for them that was right and satisfying, was all lost. Not only did they lose it all, but they became enslaved by the author of death and his plan is always to steal, kill, and destroy. So, from that time, the Bible began to tell us the history of humanity and how far they fell from God.

Sometimes it's called "the fall" because, really, they fell from the high status that they were created to live and function in. After all, without God, they couldn't do it. It was not possible. So, they fell, and in that decline, everything that was right was reversed and has been ever since.

Instead of living in blessing, they lived in fear and jealousy. One of Adam and Eve's sons even killed their other son. Because of sin, we see war, insecurity, animosity, injustice, inequity, and racism. The strong rule the weak. The rich rule the poor. There's a division between nationalities and tribes.

You could probably think of people that you really just don't like because they're a 'this' or a 'that' or a certain color or speak a certain language or from a certain tribe or an area of the world. Or, maybe they're in a certain life circumstance and you hate that. There are so many things that go on in humanity, all as a result of sin. Sin entered the human family and that sin is what separates people from God. So, when you study human history, you see that societies began to develop and religions began to be created. All kinds of things developed, and in the midst of all of human development, look around at the world as it is. There are two things that are so obvious.

There are many religions; different ways that people are searching for God. They feel empty. You probably go to sleep at night and you have questions. You have fears, things you may not tell anyone, but it's going on in you. There's something you know isn't right, and you see that, so people search for a fix for that. Sometimes, they search in alcohol, drugs, or sex. Sometimes, they search by chasing success or by seeking power or prestige. The other thing that you see is great division. Just look at the division of nations and tribes and economic categories; everything is divided.

So, you really study what has happened to humanity. You wonder, "Well, is there any hope? Is there any hope for me? This God who loved me and created me - what did He do to teach us? Did He become angry? What was His response? Did He want revenge? Did He want to punish? What did He want? How did He deal with this?"

Christ's Substitution

Well, that's really the good news, and that brings us to the part of the story that begins to give us hope. With this news, we can live in this life with great hope for now and for eternity, and that's what we call Christ's substitution. According to the scriptures, God knew the condition of humanity. The Bible says that God saw it, and He didn't like it, so He, Himself, came, and He wrapped himself in the flesh of a human person that we know as Jesus Christ. He's a historic figure, people know about Him, but, according to the Bible, He came as a baby, born of a virgin. That was God wrapped in flesh.

Can you imagine that the God who was able to create everything that exists - the sun, the moon, the stars, every river, every ocean, humanity, everything - would surrender himself? Everyone sinned. There's not one who could be clean or without sin, and God came like one of us. Think of it this way. When I say that we've all sinned, that somehow seems harsh because you see an innocent newborn baby and you think, "That baby's never sinned." Yet I have seen women who go to prison because, let's say, for example, they've committed a crime that, according to the laws of their land, is punishable by imprisonment and ultimate death. Yet when they are in that prison, they become pregnant. It happens all the time. When that baby is born, where is the baby born? Well, the baby is born in prison. Had that baby done anything wrong? No, but because of the condition of the mother, the guilt of the mother, and the circumstance that she lived in, her offspring was born in that same condition.

That's the way that each of us was really born into the condition of sin, and we've lived that way our whole lives. Do you think that baby grows up to learn to be good and kind and generous? Oh, no. It learns to behave just like a prisoner, angry and fighting and scheming, becoming just like the other prisoners. Why? Because that's the environment. That's the way that we are. We learn to hate. We learn to get even. We learn to be afraid in the environments in which we're born.

Instead, God came into our prison. He had done nothing wrong. Jesus was perfect as the Son of God, God in flesh. I love that about Him. That tells you so much about God and how much He loves you because He was willing to come like the worst of us, He walked among people without sin and, while He walked among us, He taught us things that we had never heard before.

He taught that God wants to be our Father and that He loves us, and that we can love one another. We can forgive one another. We can be forgiven and we can have a new life, have a new citizenship, and be part of the Kingdom of God and the plan of God. Think about it. We can be delivered from everything that we were enslaved by. We can be delivered from our fears, our addictions, our past, and all the mistakes that we've made. All that could go away. Jesus taught us that, but, of course, the big question was how.

How could that be? Well, in the Christ substitution part of the story, we understand that Jesus Christ, the Son of God, came with an ultimate mission. This is really beyond our logic. It's beyond our human understanding, but Jesus Christ died on the cross and was punished as a criminal although he was sinless. In that dying, according to the Bible, He took on Himself the sin of the world - yours, mine, everyone's - and He paid the full punishment.

We were guilty. We deserved to die. It's just like that woman that was in prison because of her crime. Imagine if, one day, a jailer comes and says, "The judge has said that you can walk out now. You're free." She would wonder, "Who's playing with me? This is not rational. I'm guilty. I deserve this punishment." Then she's told, "No, someone else has paid your penalty. Someone else has served your sentence so that you are no longer guilty. This is the way it is."

When Christ suffered our punishment, He died on the cross. His blood was shed for the sins of the world. After He died, they took him off the cross. They put Him in a grave. It looked like His life was over. His mission was partially over, but not completely because the best news of all is that He came out of the grave. After 3 days, He came out of the grave, and when He came out; think about this. He went into the grave with the sins of the world on Him, with the lashes on His body that represented our sins and everything that's broken about us, everything that's not perfect the way God intended us to be. All of that was on Him. The Bible says that His body was so marked that He wasn't recognizable as a man. Scripture talks about His body being like a plowed field. Imagine the suffering.

You see, that was for us. He was innocent. When you look at the suffering of Christ, you know how bad our sins were and what we really deserved. Instead, God took it on Himself through Christ and went into the grave. When He came out of the grave my friend, He didn't have any of that with Him. No sin was on Him. No sickness was on Him. No depression, no anger, no fear, no resentment, no injustice; none of the bruises and the things that shrink us in life and oppress us were on Him. None of the things that try to destroy our lives and that do destroy many lives were on Him. So, you see, Jesus is alive, and when He came out of the grave, He came out in great victory. He had conquered death, and since He conquered death, He conquered it not for Himself. He was God. He conquered it for us.

What kind of death am I talking about? I'm talking about spiritual death, the same death that separated us from God. Through Jesus, by believing in Him and accepting Him into our lives, acknowledging Him as the sacrifice for our sin and the Savior of the world, by allowing Him to come in, we are forever changed. The Bible calls that being born again, and when we're born again, we're starting over. It's a new life. It's a brand-new way of life. We give Jesus all of our old problems and our old life, and we take His new life.

Our Restoration

When we take His life, we take a life of victory, help, purpose, righteousness, and perfection. We become like Him. Isn't that amazing? I can't explain how that happens. It happened to me. I know thousands of people who have had it happen to them and the secret is this. Remember that I told you that Adam and Eve made a choice that took them away from God? When Jesus comes to you and you hear what I'm telling you now, that's what we call hearing the good news of Jesus. We have to respond. We make a choice, that's the key. You can't just hear it and walk away. You have to make a choice.

It is wonderful to make a choice to turn away from your old life and way of living and turn back to God through Jesus Christ. Now, when that happens, the Scripture talks about us becoming new creations and being born again. The old passes away and all things become new. That's what we call our restoration. You see, our restoration is what happens from the time that we accept Jesus Christ, and allow Him into our lives. From that moment, we learn how to live this new way of life.

You see, if Adam and Eve had never left the garden, we would have grown in that atmosphere knowing how to live as children of God, but we learned how to live as sinful people. When we come back, through Christ to God's family, now we learn how to live as God's children. That's the new life, our restoration. It's not just being saved so that we are free from our sin and our punishment. It's more than that. It's that now we live as new people. It's hard to believe, but we accept it by faith so that the drunkard becomes the righteous man, and the thief becomes a wonderful businessperson. The prostitute becomes an honorable woman. Even a carrier of this message - you don't know what my background has been, but when Jesus came, my life became new. So, the past is gone. I, then, have the privilege of sharing God's love, the love of Jesus, and what He did. I have the privilege of giving you the chance to choose to believe in Him and receive His new life. So, make the choice. Choose Jesus, and I'll help you pray and receive Him right now.

Thoughts About the Gospel Icon

- The Gospel Icon method of sharing the Gospel has the advantage of highlighting the devil and his role in messing up the world. Many of the other methods of sharing the Gospel focus on the message that man is a sinner without including the fact that we are in a cosmic battle between good and evil. God is good and the devil is bad and much of the evil in the world is not only caused by man's sinfulness but is also caused by an evil foe who is actively trying to steal, kill, and destroy.

- Every message on healing, prosperity, and marriage should start in God's creation. We start with God's original plan, then we move into how God's plan was messed up by Satan. Then, we talk about how the cross brings correction, and finish by talking about our restoration to God's plan.

- Outline of The Gospel Icon:

1. The Tree of Life represents God's creation.

- God's Plan
- Dignity
- Equality
- Purpose
- Beautiful, plentiful, harmonious, perfect

2. The Serpent evokes Satan's Deception.

- Satan's Plan. There was an enemy. His deception convinced Adam and Eve to accept a lie instead of the truth.
- Shame
- Deception
- Fear

- Some preachers focus too much on Satan's role. Some preachers have lots of sermons on sin.
- Satan misquoted God.

3. The Cross portrays Christ's Substitution.

- With His own arm, He brought salvation for us.
- Forgiveness instead of shame
- Relationship instead of separation.
- Peace instead of fear

4. The New Blossom signifies Our Restoration.

- Yes, He suffered. Yes, He died. But what does it do for me in my pain and in my suffering?
- Restored to Dignity
- Restored to Equality
- Restored to Purpose

CHAPTER 4

THE THREE CIRCLES

Key Scriptures: *"For I know the plans I have for you," declares the Lord, "plans to prosper you and not to harm you, plans to give you hope and a future. Then you will call on me and come and pray to me, and I will listen to you. You will seek me and find me when you seek me with all your heart"* (Jeremiah 29:11-13 NIV).

The Three Circles

Source: Jimmy Scroggins, lead pastor of the First Baptist Church of West Palm Beach, Florida, developed this as a witnessing tool for his congregation.[8]

WHAT TO SAY:

The First Circle Represents God's Design

I believe God has a perfect design for every area of our lives. God has a plan for our families, our marriages, our sex lives, our money, our work life, and even our entertainment. God has a design for every area of our lives.

The Run Away Man

The problem is that something inside us wants to do things our own way instead of following God's plan. Far too often, we run away from God's perfect design. The Bible has a word to describe running away from God's design and that word is "sin."

8 Jimmy Scroggins, "3 Circles Training - Lesson 2 - The Gospel", (Accessed February 3, 2023), https://www.youtube.com/watch?v=7f3FR127NcQ

The Second Circle Represents Brokenness

When people sin against God's design, they end up in a place of brokenness. This is tragic because brokenness really hurts. The brokenness of human life is real and is something that every person can relate to. Whether you go to church every Sunday or whether you have never gone to church your entire life, you probably know what it is like to experience brokenness, either because of your own choices or because of the choices of someone who has hurt you. Brokenness can come from bad relationships or from something internal. People can get addicted, depressed, discouraged, and worried. They can feel used or they feel empty.

The Crooked Lines

When people find themselves in a place of brokenness, they look for a way to fix themselves. We start looking for a solution to the pain we feel. We go on a search for a way to numb the pain, escape the depressed feeling, and get out of the place of brokenness. The problem is that we just get more and more broken. The feeling of brokenness lets us know that something needs to change. The feeling of being messed up, frustrated, and disgusted with life drives us to look for change. But, after we try different ways to escape the brokenness, we quickly realize that we can't change ourselves, and we start looking for someone to help us change.

The Praying Man

The Bible actually has a word for change and that is the word "repent." When we come to a point where we realize that we cannot change ourselves, we realize that we need God's help. This feeling drives us to our knees to ask God to help us change.

The Third Circle Represents God's Plan of Salvation

The Bible has a solution for the problem of brokenness and it's called "The Gospel." Gospel is a Bible word that means "good news." This is the good news, that God loves us so much that when He sees us in our brokenness, He does not leave us there. Two thousand years ago, He sent His own Son Jesus to come and live a perfect life. Jesus never departed from God's perfect design. Jesus never sinned. He loved people. He cared about people. He healed people who were hurting, and He spoke up for people who were broken.

But one day, when Jesus was about 33 years old, some evil men crucified Him on a cross. They put nails in His hands and feet and a crown of thorns on His head. When Jesus was hanging on the cross,

God put the sins of the whole world on Jesus, including your sins and my sins. His body was broken so that our broken lives could be fixed.

Jesus died on the cross, but He did not stay dead. The good news is that after three days, Jesus rose from the dead. This miracle resurrection proved that Jesus is the Son of God and that He has the power to forgive our sins.

The Rejoicing Man

So, if we truly want to experience change, we have to believe in Jesus. The Bible's word for believing in Jesus is the word "faith." We have to believe that Jesus rose from the dead and we have to put our faith and trust in Him. By faith, we believe that Jesus is our Savior and that He can rescue us from our brokenness.

When we turn away from our sins and turn to Jesus, God does a miracle in our lives. He restores us to His original plan for our lives and we become whole. When we cry out to Jesus, He fixes everything that is broken and gives us the ability to pursue God's perfect design for our lives.

Even if you are one thousand steps away from God, He is only one step back. No matter what you have done, what mistakes you have made or how broken your life is, God is waiting for you. Once you become a believer in Jesus, you come full circle all the way back to God's perfect design for your life.

Please, use this illustration to share "good news" with the people around you! The Bible has a word for a person who shares "good news", and that word is "evangelist." That's what I am and what you can be too.

Thoughts About the Three Circles

- I like this illustration so much that I printed some stickers to put on the back of my cell phone so that I would have a Gospel presentation ready to share everywhere I go. I find the illustration non-threatening. I ask people, "Have you ever seen this picture before?" Most people respond by trying to figure out what the strange hieroglyphics mean. This gives me the opportunity to launch into the explanation of the Gospel.

- The Three Circles begins by talking about God's perfect design for our lives instead of talking about our flaws that are caused by sin. The idea that God has a plan for our marriages, our sex lives, and even our money is a radical idea nowadays. Our society wants to do things our way instead of God's way. It is the running away from God's plan that has caused so many problems in our society.

- I like the way that this script gives a definition for Christian words. In an increasingly post-Christian society, we cannot assume that people know what words like sin, repentance, and faith mean. By giving a simple definition of these words, we can ensure that our listener understands what we are saying.

- Recently we hosted a Free Prayer booth at the Tulsa State Fair. As people walked by our booth, we offered to pray for them. I used the Three Circles Illustration to present the Gospel to the children.

The results were amazing! Here are some of the numbers that tell the story:

- 11 Days of Outreach
- 132 Hours of Ministry
- We engaged in a total of 1,001 conversations about God.
- Our team prayed with 1,844 people.
- We led 479 people in a prayer of salvation.
- 60 people testified they received physical healing.
- A total of 318 volunteers came to help us pray.
- 2 Sunday morning church services for Carnival workers.

Many of our volunteers at the Free Prayer booth were teenagers or college students who had never had the opportunity to lead a person to Christ before. We used the Free Prayer booth and the Three Circles Illustration as a way to train these young people how to share their faith. Now that they have seen God move through them, they will continue to be bold in telling people about Jesus.

CHAPTER 5

THE THREE GREATEST EVENTS IN THE BIBLE

Key Scriptures: Genesis 1:1, I Corinthians 13:3-4, Acts 1:8

The Three Greatest Events in the Bible

Creation
God Created You!
God The Father's
Greatest Work

Calvary
God Saves You!
God the Son's
Greatest Work

Pentecost
God Empowers You!
God the Holy Spirit's
Greatest Work

Source: Daniel King

WHAT TO SAY:

I often preach this sermon on the mission field. Below are my sermon notes on how I share this message.

Miracle #1: God Created Me! – Creation

Everyone raise your hand in the air and say, "God created me!"

At the beginning of time, God created the heavens and the earth. Everything that you can see was created by God. God created the birds. He created the plants. He created the animals and He created a man and a woman. The first man and woman were named Adam and Eve.

Everything that God created has a purpose. The birds were made to fly. The plants were made to give us food. God also created Adam and Eve with a purpose. He created them to be His friends. Every day, God would walk and talk with Adam and Eve. You were created with the same purpose. God created you to be His friend. He wants to walk and talk with you every day.

Everything that God created is beautiful. God does not create trash. He does not create junk. God created you and God made you beautiful. You are so good-looking. You are good-looking because God created you that way. God created you with great value. You are so valuable to God.

God created Adam and Eve and every day God would walk and talk with them. But, one day, Adam and Eve sinned. What is sin? Sin is when we disobey God's commands. God says that you must not lie. But, we lie. God says that you must not steal. But, humans steal. God says that you must "love your brother," yet humans have hate in their hearts.

Since Adam and Eve sinned, they were separated from God. Their fellowship with God was broken. They could not walk and talk with God any longer. The Bible says, "all have sinned." Every person has done things that are wrong.

For thousands of years, mankind has tried to restore fellowship with God. Some people think that if they can get rich enough, they can buy a place in heaven, but riches will not save you. Other people think that if they study hard and become really smart, they can find salvation, but no matter how smart you are, you cannot figure out how to be saved by yourself. Others try to get to God through religious rituals, but religious rituals will not save you. No matter how hard we try, it is impossible for us to cross the gap between us and God because our sin separates us from God.

The Bible says, "the price for sin is death, but the gift of God is eternal life through Jesus Christ our Lord."

Miracle #2: God Saves Me! – Calvary

Raise your hand in the air and say, "God Saves Me!"

Man cannot get to God, and because of that, God came here to us. God sent His only Son to earth to become a man. His name was Jesus.

Jesus was born to a virgin named Mary. He grew up and walked the dusty streets of Israel. Jesus had disciples. Every day Jesus would take the disciples by the hand and He would walk and talk with them. He fellowshipped with the disciples. Jesus did many miracles. He healed the sick. He opened the eyes of the blind. The cripples came to Jesus. He touched the cripples and suddenly they could walk.

Then some evil men came, and they crucified Jesus on a cross. They put nails in the hands of Jesus. They put nails in His feet. They hung Him on the cross. It was a horrible punishment, but Jesus did not deserve to be punished. He was the Son of God. He did nothing wrong, but He died on the cross. The reason He died was to be a sacrifice for your sin. Every person has sinned, but Jesus died on the cross to pay the price for our sins. He did not deserve to die, but He stretched out His arms and He gave His life so that you could live and be forgiven.

Jesus did not stay dead on the cross. After three days, Jesus rose from the dead, and today, Jesus is alive. Jesus is not dead; Jesus is not in a tomb. Jesus is alive today.

Everyone shout, "Jesus is Alive!"

Because Jesus died on the cross, we can be forgiven of all our sin! The Bible says that "the blood of Jesus cleanses us from all sin."

What can wash away sin from the human heart? If you do something wrong, can you wash away guilt with soap? No. The only thing that can wash away sin is the blood of Jesus. Jesus died on the cross to save you from your sins. The Bible says, "everyone who calls on the name of Jesus shall be saved." How can your sins be forgiven? You must call on the name of Jesus. Jesus forgives your sins.

If you will cry out to Jesus, He will save you from every sin. He will wash your sins away and He will give you a brand-new life. He will restore your fellowship with God. When you die, you will go to heaven instead of hell.

The greatest miracle is the one that happens when Jesus saves you. God created you, but because of sin, you are broken. Because Jesus died on the cross, you can be saved. If you will cry out to Jesus, Jesus will forgive your sins and He will make you a brand-new creation.

How many of you want Jesus to save you today? Lift your hand if you want to be saved. I am going to pray, and I want you to repeat this prayer after me. We are going to ask God to forgive our sins and when we do, He will save you from every sin.

I will say this prayer first, then you repeat after me. Everyone say, "Dear God in Heaven, I cry out to Jesus. Jesus, save me. I believe that Jesus died on the cross. I believe that Jesus rose from the dead. Jesus, you are my Lord. In the name of Jesus, Amen."

Everyone raise your hand and say, "Jesus saves me!"

Miracle #3: God Empowers Me! – Pentecost

After Jesus rose from the dead, He went up into heaven. But before He went up into heaven, He promised the disciples, "I will send you a comforter. I will send you a helper." The name of this helper is the Holy Spirit. The Holy Spirit will come and live inside you, and every day, you will be able to walk and talk with God.

The Holy Spirit wants to walk and talk with you every single day.

Now, I want to pray for you to be filled with the power of the Holy Spirit. If you want to be filled with the Holy Spirit, lift your hands into the air and repeat this prayer, "Dear God in Heaven, I invite you to walk with me and talk with me every day. I need the Holy Spirit. Holy Spirit, fill me with your power. In Jesus' name, Amen."

Everyone raise your hand and say, "God Empowers Me!"

Thoughts About the Three Greatest Events in the Bible

- This is a sermon that I preach regularly. It is useful for providing a picture of the overall story of the Bible. This message establishes a Christian worldview for those who have not been exposed to it before.

- In the first miracle, we see God the Father's greatest work which is creation. In the second great miracle, we see God the Son's greatest work which is salvation. In the third greatest miracle, we see the Holy Spirit's ongoing work of empowering the believer.

- This Gospel presentation is easy to remember, simple to present, and covers the full story of the Bible.

- Of all of the Gospel presentations, this is the only one that mentions the Holy Spirit. This makes this outline an ideal presentation for Pentecostals to use.

| CHAPTER 6 |

THE ROMANS ROAD

Key Scriptures: Romans 3:10-18, Romans 3:23, Romans 5:1, Romans 5:8, Romans 6:23, Romans 8:1, Romans 8:38-39, Romans 10:9-10, Romans 10:13.

The Romans Road

Source: The Romans Road is commonly found in witnessing literature.

WHAT TO SAY:

First Stop on the Romans Road: The Reality of Sin

Romans 3:23 *"for all have sinned and fall short of the glory of God."*

This verse tells us that all have sinned. No one is perfect because we have all disobeyed God's commands. God is holy and we are not. The word "sin" means "to miss the mark." If I shoot an arrow at a target, my goal is to hit the bullseye. Sometimes, an archer might just be happy he hit the target, but really, a perfect shot is hitting the bullseye right in the center of the target. To go to heaven, we have to hit the bullseye with every shot. According to this verse, everyone, without exception, misses the mark. We have all done something wrong.

We sin because it is human nature to sin, and we sin by choice. Many times, people do not want to admit that they are sinners because they have never killed anyone. Yet sin is not measured against another person who has done something "worse" than us. Our imperfections are measured against the standards of a perfect and holy God. None of us are perfect in every thought and action.

Romans 3:10-18 provides a picture of what sin looks like in our lives: *"As it is written: "There is none righteous, no, not one; There is none who understands; There is none who seeks after God. They have all turned aside; They have together become unprofitable; There is none who does good, no, not one." "Their throat is an open tomb; With their tongues they have practiced deceit"; "The poison of asps is under their lips";" Whose mouth is full of cursing and bitterness." "Their feet are swift to shed blood; Destruction and misery are in their ways; And the way of peace they have not known." "There is no fear of God before their eyes."*

This verse gives us a detailed picture of what sin looks like. Sin is ugly. Sin causes a lack of peace. Sin destroys God's perfect plan.

Second Stop on the Romans Road: The Cost of Sin

Romans 6:23 *"For the wages of sin is death, but the gift of God is eternal life in Christ Jesus our Lord."*

When a person does something wrong, there is always a price to be paid. In natural terms, a disobedient child is spanked by his parents, a thief is thrown into jail, and a murderer is executed. Disobeying God's commands has a price that must be paid. The price for sin is death. However, even though we deserve to die because of our sins, God has made a way for us to be redeemed.

Third Stop on the Romans Road: The Payment for Sin

Romans 5:8 *"But God demonstrates His own love toward us, in that while we were still sinners, Christ died for us."*

We deserve to die because of our sins, but Christ died in our place. Jesus' death paid the price for our sins and His resurrection proves that God accepted His death as payment for our sins. Jesus was able to be a perfect sacrifice for our sins because He lived a perfect life.

Fourth Stop on the Romans Road: The Way to Salvation

Romans 10:9 *"If you confess with your mouth the Lord Jesus and believe in your heart that God has raised Him from the dead, you will be saved."*

Romans 10:13 *For "whoever calls on the name of the Lord shall be saved."*

Salvation is a free gift given to everyone who asks for it. We cannot earn salvation, we accept it. A response to Jesus is required. You must do more than understand God's plan of salvation, you have to act on your understanding.

When a husband and wife get married, they make vows to one another. They promise to love one another. If a groom refused to repeat a vow of love to his bride, the wedding would be called off. Confessing Jesus with your mouth is like making a wedding vow. You use your mouth to confess you want Jesus to be your Lord and Savior.

Fifth Stop on the Romans Road: Results of Salvation

Romans 5:1 *"Therefore, having been justified by faith, we have peace with God through our Lord Jesus Christ..."*

The word "justified" means "to be made righteous" or "to be right with God." Faith means to put your trust in Jesus for salvation. Through Jesus Christ, we can have a peaceful relationship with God. One of the biggest problems in the world today is a lack of peace. Turning to Jesus will bring peace to your heart.

Sixth Stop on the Romans Road: Benefit of Salvation

Romans 8:1 *"There is therefore now no condemnation to those who are in Christ Jesus, who do not walk according to the flesh, but according to the Spirit."*

Even though we have sinned in the past, once we come to Jesus, there is no longer any condemnation. The word "condemnation" means "to express strong disapproval." God is not sitting in heaven looking for a way to judge you. No. Once you come to Jesus you are forgiven and free from sin.

Seventh Stop on the Romans Road: Assurance of Salvation

Romans 8:38-39 *"For I am persuaded that neither death nor life, nor angels nor principalities nor powers, nor things present nor things to* *come, nor height nor depth, nor any other created thing, shall be able to separate us from the love of God which is in Christ Jesus our Lord."*

Do you want to follow the Roman's Road to Salvation? If so, repeat this simple prayer. The prayer itself will not save you; it is by putting your faith in Jesus Christ that you will be saved. Repeating this prayer is a way for you to tell God that you are trusting in Jesus Christ for your salvation.

"Dear God in Heaven, I am a sinner. I have fallen short of Your perfect standard. I believe Jesus died on the cross to pay for my sins. Today, I repent of every sin. I call on Jesus to be saved. I confess that Jesus is my Lord. I believe in my heart that God has raised Jesus from the dead. God, please give me Your peace. I am no longer subject to the condemnation of sin because I am in Christ Jesus. I believe nothing can separate me from the love of God because I am saved. In Jesus' name, Amen."

Thoughts About the Romans Road

- The Romans Road has been around for a long time, and some have criticized it simply because it is old. Yet, if you ever go to the city of Rome, you will find roads still in use that were made before the time of Christ. Just because something is ancient does not mean it is ineffective.[9]

- The Romans Road to Salvation is a simple but powerful way of presenting the good news of salvation by only using verses that are found in the book of Romans. You can sit down with a friend, open up your Bible to the book of Romans, and take them through all the major points of the Gospel without ever leaving the book. These verses explain why people need sal-

9 Joe Oden, Empowered to Share, (Dallas, TX: Joe Oden Ministries, 2020), 86.

vation, how God provides salvation, how to receive salvation, and the results of receiving salvation.

- When a person asks, "How can I be saved?" the Romans Road is a great way to lead them to salvation. I recommend highlighting each of these Scriptures in your Bible and next to each verse, write the reference of the next verse in the sequence. By doing this, you do not have to remember all the references. All you need to know is the starting point. Once you begin, you can make your way through the entire presentation.

- The Romans Road is an easy way to communicate God's plan of salvation, but it does not do justice to the full thrust of Paul's emphasis in the book of Romans.[10] It is like digging up a few paving stones from Paul's road and presenting them as the whole thing. Or, it is like taking six pearls from a string of pearls and admiring them without looking at the whole necklace. The book of Romans contains deep theology, and it deserves to be studied in its fullness.

- The book of Romans is about more than a personal narrative of salvation. It involves the in-breaking of a Creator God into Jewish history in order to make Christ Lord of all, both Jew and Gentile.

---

10 Andrew Perriman, "What's wrong with the "Romans Road" to Salvation?", Accessed February 3, 2023, https://www.postost.net/2012/05/what-s-wrong-romans-road-salvation

CHAPTER 7

THE STEPS TO SALVATION

The Romans Road is well-known and well-traveled. However, the same elements of the Gospel that are found on the Romans Road can also be discovered in other books of the Bible.

The main elements of the Gospel are:

1. The Reality of Sin
2. The Judgement for Sin
3. Christ Died for Our Sins
4. You Can Accept Christ by Faith

In the next few pages, I want to share with you new highways for witnessing. These include Isaiah's Itinerary, John's Journey, Hebrews' Highway, the Ephesians Expressway, First John's Freeway, and Revelation's Route to Salvation. I encourage you to become familiar with sharing the Gospel from several different books in the Bible. As you become adept at sharing the Gospel, you can mix and match verses from these different books.

Some might ask, "Why would I want to use these different pathways to communicate the Gospel?" If you met the Ethiopian Eunuch and only had the book of Isaiah to refer to in a pinch or you were talking to a Jew, you might see a reason to use the book of

The Steps to Salvation

	Isaiah	John	Hebrews	Eph 2:1-10	1 John	Revelation
Step #1: The Reality of Sin 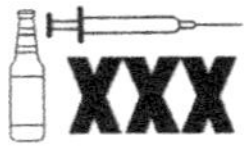	Isaiah 53:6	John 3:18	Hebrews 10:26	*...the lusts of our flesh,..*	1 John 5:16	Revelation 21:8
Step #2: The Judgement for Sin 	Isaiah 53:12	John 3:36	Hebrews 10:27-31	*...dead in trespasses and sins*	1 John 4:9	Revelation 21:8
Step #3: Christ Died for Our Sins 	Isaiah 53:4-10	John 3:16	Hebrews 10:10-12	*God, who is rich in mercy, because of His great love with which He loved us...made us alive together with Christ*	1 John 4:16	Revelation 5:12
Step #4: You Can Accept Christ by Faith 	Isaiah 53:4-10	John 1:12	Hebrews 11:6	*For by grace you have been saved through faith,*	1 John 5:13	Revelation 3:20
Bonus Verse: 	Accept Christ by Faith Isaiah 55:6-7	Jesus the Way to Salvation John 14:6				

Isaiah. Otherwise, why not use a more obvious book of the Bible, like the classic Romans Road? The reason I present these different roads through Scripture is that if one sees an idea once in Scripture, one knows it is important, but if the same thought is presented many different times and in many different books of the Bible, it increases in importance. When we see these ideas presented in book after book throughout the Bible, the repetition of this outline becomes more significant. God's plan of salvation is bigger than the book of Romans. His plan is actually found in many different parts of Scripture.

Isaiah's Itinerary to Salvation

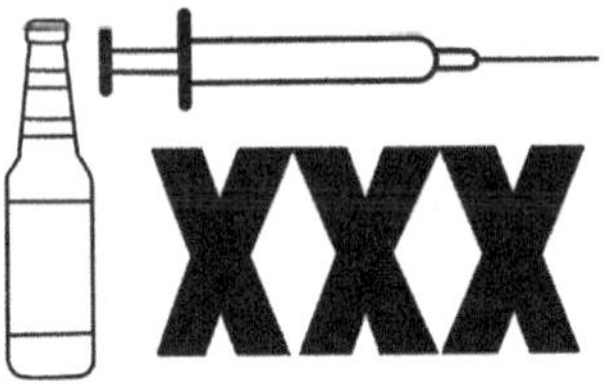

Step #1: The Reality of Sin - Isaiah 53:6 *"All we like sheep have gone astray; We have turned, every one, to his own way; And the Lord has laid on Him the iniquity of us all"*

Step #2: The Judgement for Sin - Isaiah 53:12 *"...Because He poured out His soul unto death, And He was numbered with the transgressors, And He bore the sin of many, And made intercession for the transgressors."*

Step #3: Christ Died for Our Sins - Isaiah 53:4-10 *"Surely He has borne our griefs And carried our sorrows; Yet we esteemed Him stricken, Smitten by God, and afflicted. But He was wounded for our transgressions, He was bruised for our iniquities; The chastisement for our*

peace was upon Him, And by His stripes we are healed. All we like sheep have gone astray; We have turned, every one, to his own way; And the Lord has laid on Him the iniquity of us all. He was oppressed and He was afflicted, Yet He opened not His mouth; He was led as a lamb to the slaughter, And as a sheep before its shearers is silent, So He opened not His mouth. He was taken from prison and from judgment, And who will declare His generation? For He was cut off from the land of the living; For the transgressions of My people He was stricken. And they made His grave with the wicked— But with the rich at His death, Because He had done no violence, Nor was any deceit in His mouth. Yet it pleased the Lord to bruise Him; He has put Him to grief. When You make His soul an offering for sin, He shall see His seed, He shall prolong His days, And the pleasure of the Lord shall prosper in His hand."

Step #4: You Can Accept Christ by Faith - Isaiah 55:6-7 *"Seek the Lord while He may be found, Call upon Him while He is near. Let the wicked forsake his way, And the unrighteous man his thoughts; Let him return to the Lord, And He will have mercy on him; And to our God, For He will abundantly pardon"*

John's Journey to Salvation

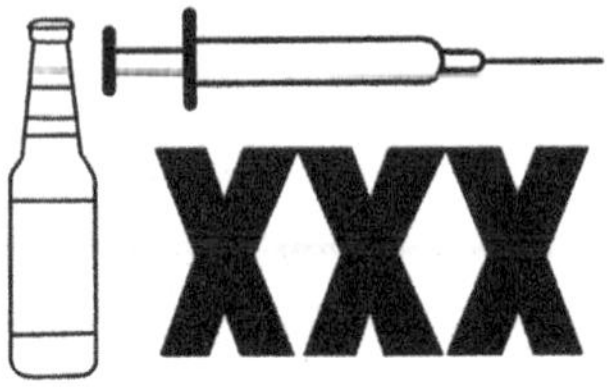

Step #1: The Reality of Sin - *"He who believes in Him is not condemned; but he who does not believe is condemned already, because he has not believed in the name of the only begotten Son of God"* (John 3:18).

Step #2: The Judgement for Sin - *"He who believes in the Son has everlasting life; and he who does not believe the Son shall not see life, but the wrath of God abides on him"* (John 3:36).

Step #3: Christ Died for Our Sins - "*For God so loved the world that He gave His only begotten Son, that whoever believes in Him should not perish but have everlasting life"* (John 3:16).

Step #4: You Can Accept Christ by Faith - *"But as many as received Him, to them He gave the right to become children of God, to those who believe in His name"* (John 1:12)

Bonus Verse: Jesus the Way to Salvation *"Jesus said to him, "I am the way, the truth, and the life. No one comes to the Father except through Me"* (John 14:6).

Hebrews' Highway to Salvation

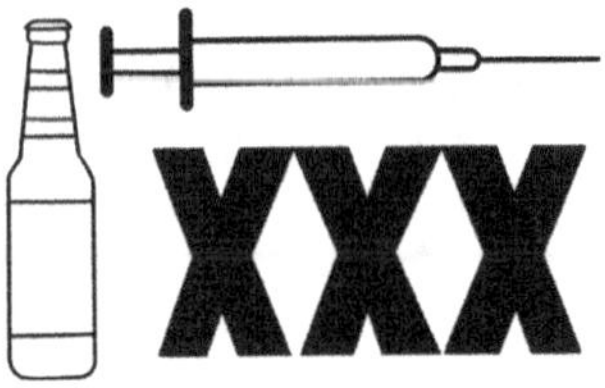

Step #1: The Reality of Sin - *"For if we sin willfully after we have received the knowledge of the truth, there no longer remains a sacrifice for sins"* (Hebrews 10:26).

Step #2: The Judgement for Sin - *"but a certain fearful expectation of judgment, and fiery indignation which will devour the adversaries. Anyone who has rejected Moses' law dies without mercy on the testimony of two or three witnesses. Of how much worse punishment, do you suppose, will he be thought worthy who has trampled the Son of God underfoot, counted the blood of the covenant by which he was sanctified a common thing, and insulted the Spirit of grace? For we know Him who said, "Vengeance is Mine, I will repay," says the Lord. And again, "The Lord will judge His people." It is a fearful thing to fall into the hands of the living God"* (Hebrews 10:27-31).

Step #3: Christ Died for Our Sins - *"By that will we have been sanctified through the offering of the body of Jesus Christ once for all. And every priest stands ministering daily and offering repeatedly the same sacrifices, which can never take away sins. But this Man, after He had offered one sacrifice for sins forever, sat down at the right hand of God"* (Hebrews 10:10-12).

Step #4: You Can Accept Christ by Faith - *"But without faith it is impossible to please Him, for he who comes to God must believe that He is, and that He is a rewarder of those who diligently seek Him"* (Hebrews 11:6).

Ephesians' Expressway to Salvation

If I wanted to present the Gospel with only one passage, I would bring people to these verses in the book of Ephesians. It is a one-stop location for salvation.

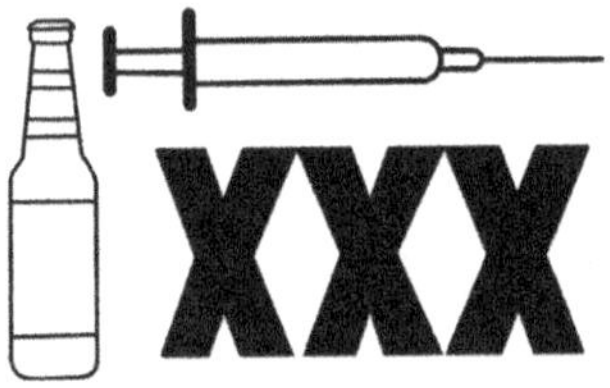

Step #1: The Reality of Sin -"*...And you He made alive, who were dead in trespasses and sins, in which you once walked according to the course of this world, according to the prince of the power of the air, the spirit who now works in the sons of disobedience...*" (Ephesians 2:1-2)

Step #2: The Judgement for Sin - "*...among whom also we all once conducted ourselves in the lusts of our flesh, fulfilling the desires of the flesh and of the mind, and were by nature children of wrath, just as the others....*" (Ephesians 2:3)

Step #3: Christ Died for Our Sins - *But God, who is rich in mercy, because of His great love with which He loved us, even when we were dead in trespasses, made us alive together with Christ (by grace you have been saved), and raised us up together, and made us sit together in the heavenly places in Christ Jesus, that in the ages to come He might show the exceeding riches of His grace in His kindness toward us in Christ Jesus.* (Ephesians 2:4-7)

Step #4: You Can Accept Christ by Faith *"…For by grace you have been saved through faith, and that not of yourselves; it is the gift of God, not of works, lest anyone should boast. For we are His workmanship, created in Christ Jesus for good works, which God prepared beforehand that we should walk in them"* (Ephesians 2:8-10).

First John's Freeway to Salvation

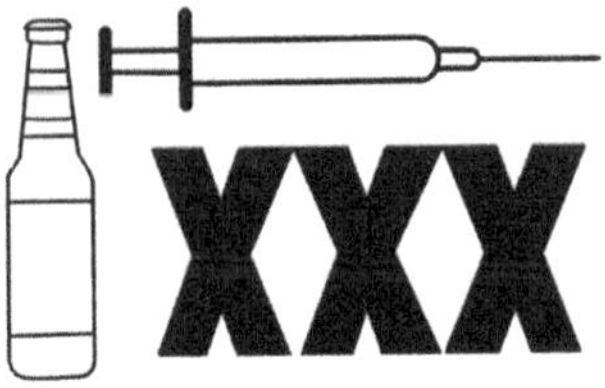

Step #1: The Reality of Sin - *"If we say that we have no sin, we deceive ourselves, and the truth is not in us. If we confess our sins, He is faithful and just to forgive us our sins and to cleanse us from all unrighteousness"* (1 John 1:8-9).

Step #2: The Judgement for Sin - "If anyone sees his brother sinning a sin *which does* not *lead* to death, he will ask, and He will give him life for those who commit sin not *leading* to death. There is sin *leading* to death. I do not say that he should pray about that" (1 John 5:16).

Step #3: Christ Died for Our Sins - *"By this we know love, because He laid down His life for us..."* (1 John 3:16). *"In this the love of God was manifested toward us, that God has sent His only begotten Son into the world, that we might live through Him"* (1 John 4:9).

Step #4: You Can Accept Christ by Faith - *"Whoever confesses that Jesus is the Son of God, God abides in him, and he in God"* (1 John 4:15) *"And we have known and believed the love that God has for us. God is love, and he who abides in love abides in God, and God in him"* (1 John 4:16).

Bonus Verse: The Assurance of Salvation *"These things I have written to you who believe in the name of the Son of God, that you may know that you have eternal life, and that you may continue to believe in the name of the Son of God"* (1 John 5:13).

Revelation's Route to Salvation

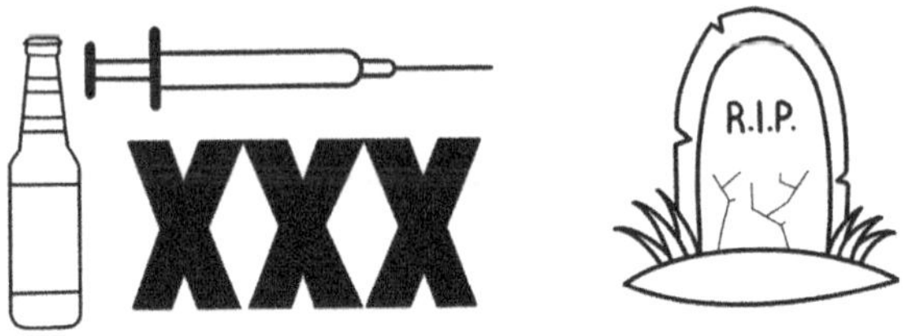

Step #1-2: The Reality of Sin and The Judgement for Sin - *"But the cowardly, unbelieving, abominable, murderers, sexually immoral, sorcerers, idolaters, and all liars shall have their part in the lake which burns with fire and brimstone, which is the second death"* (Revelation 21:8).

Step #3: Christ Died for Our Sins - *"Worthy is the Lamb who was slain To receive power and riches and wisdom, And strength and honor and glory and blessing!"* (Revelation 5:12).

Step #4: You Can Accept Christ by Faith - *"Behold, I stand at the door and knock. If anyone hears My voice and opens the door, I will come in to him and dine with him, and he with Me"* (Revelation 3:20).

| CHAPTER 8 |

TWO WAYS TO LIVE

Key Scriptures: Revelation 4:11, Romans 3:10-12, Hebrews 9:27, 1 Peter 3:18, 1 Peter 1:3, John 3:36

Two Ways to Live

Source: Matthias Media,[11] Sydney, Australia

WHAT TO SAY:

Illustration #1: God is the loving ruler of the world. He made the world. He made us rulers of the world under Him.
"You are worthy, O Lord, to receive glory and honor and power; For You created all things, And by Your will they exist and were created" (Revelation 4:11 NKJV).

Illustration #2: However, this is the way that it is now. We all reject the ruler, God, by trying to run our own life in our own way without

11 Matthias Media, "Two Ways to Live: Know and Share the Gospel Training DVD," Accessed February 3, 2023, https://youtu.be/_vBxxCor8AM, See also: Matthias Media, "Two Ways to Live," Accessed February 3, 2023, twowaystolive.com

him. But we fail to rule ourselves, society, or the world. *"There is none righteous, no, not one; There is none who understands; There is none who seeks after God. They have all turned aside"* (Romans 3:10-12).

Illustration #3: What will God do about this rebellion? God won't let us rebel forever. God's punishment for rebellion is death and judgement. *"…it is appointed for men to die once, but after this the judgment"* (Hebrews 9:27 NKJV).

Illustration #4: God's justice sounds hard, but because of His love, God sent His son into the world, the man Jesus Christ. Jesus always lived under God's rule, yet by dying in our place, He took our punishment and brought forgiveness. *"Christ also suffered once for sins, the just for the unjust, that He might bring us to God…"* (1 Peter 3:18 NKJV).

Illustration #5: But that's not all. God raised Jesus to life again as the ruler of the world. Jesus has conquered death and now gives new life and will return to judge. *"According to His abundant mercy has begotten us again to a living hope through the resurrection of Jesus Christ from the dead..."* (1 Peter 1:3).

Illustration #6: Well, where does that leave us? There are two ways to live.

1. Our way: reject the ruler, God, and try to live life our own way. What is the result? We will be condemned by God, facing death and judgment.

2. God's new way: Submit to Jesus as our ruler and rely on Jesus' death and resurrection. What is the result? We will be forgiven by God and given eternal life. *"He who believes in the Son has everlasting life; and he who does not believe the Son shall not see life, but the wrath of God abides on him"* (John 3:36 NKJV).

Which of these two choices represents the way that you want to live?

Thoughts about The Two Ways to Live

- Two Ways to Live[12] was developed to present the Gospel to college students in Sydney, Australia in the 1980s. It is easy to learn, and the pictures are easy to draw. People who are running away from God may identify as a rebel who needs to submit to God's rule.

- The main Gospel metaphors used in this presentation are:[13]
    - The Kingship of God
    - Sin is rebellion against the King.
    - The judgment for sin is a punishment from the King.
    - Jesus is the King who died for our sins.
    - The Christian life starts with submission to the King.

- The focus on God as King is a good metaphor, but it does not emphasize other aspects of God being Creator, Father, Shepherd, or Friend. The emphasis is not on the joy of the Christian life but on submission to the King.

- In a post-modern context, this metaphor does not work as well because post-moderns tend to reject authority. There is often anger against God for His arbitrary rules that take away people's freedoms. The heroes of our post-modern thinking are the American patriots who overthrew King George of England during the American revolution or Braveheart who cried "Freedom."14

---

12 Sam Chan, *Evangelism in a Skeptical World,* (Grand Rapids, MI: Zondervan, 2018), 86-89.

13 Sam Chan, *Evangelism in a Skeptical World,* 88.

14 Sam Chan, *Evangelism in a Skeptical World,* 86.

CHAPTER 9

THE ABC'S OF SALVATION

Key Verses: Romans 3:23; 6:23; Acts 3:19; 1 John 1:9, John 3:16; 15:6; Romans 5:8. Romans 10:9-10, 13

The ABC's of Salvation

Source: Dave Earley and David Wheeler[15]

WHAT TO SAY:

A - Admit that you're a sinner and that no matter what good deeds you do, you cannot earn God's love and forgiveness. Key Verses: Luke 18:9-14, Romans 3:23; 6:23; Acts 3:19; 1 John 1:9

Here's the bad news. We all have a problem. It's called sin. No one is perfect. No one is living a life in the way that God intended us to live. The consequence of sin is eternal death.

B - Believe that Jesus is God's Son and that Jesus died on the cross to save us from our sins. Believe that He rose from the dead on the third day and is alive today. Key Verses: John 3:16; 15:6; Romans 5:8.

Here is the good news. God loves us so much that He can forgive any sin, no matter how big or small. God sent His son Jesus to die

15 Dave Earley and David Wheeler, Evangelism Is… (Nashville, TN: B & H Academic Publishing, 2010), 334.

on the cross to save us from sin. Jesus promises us that if we put our trust in Him, He will save us from our sin.

C

C - Confess your faith in Christ. Key Verses: Romans 10:9-10, 13

When Jesus rose from the dead, He proved His victory over eternal death. God wants you to confess (that means to "say with your mouth") that Jesus is Lord. He is your Savior.

D

D - Do everything Jesus has commanded you. Key Verses: Matthew 7:21, Matthew 28:20.

Now that you have decided to ask Jesus to forgive your sins, it is time to live for Him. The Bible gives us instructions on how to live the God kind of way.

Thoughts About the ABC's of Salvation

- The ABCs of Salvation are typically known as Admit, Believe, Confess, and Do. Technically, these four points are not the Gospel. Rather, they are the Biblical responses a person should have to the Gospel. It is important not to rush the Gospel presentation when the ABCs are presented. For example, when one is ministering to children, the temptation is to rush right to the end in order to get the kids to make a verbal commitment to Christ, but it is important to communicate the complete message of Christ's redemption including creation, the fall, and how Christ saves us.

- A+B+C = Salvation + D = Sanctification

- After I teach school children about the ABCs of Salvation, I ask them to repeat after me using numbers to help them remember what Jesus has done for them:

1-2-3 "Repeat after me," 5-6-7 "Now you go to heaven," 8-9-10, "You are born-again!"

CHAPTER 10

THE HAND

Key Verses: Romans 3:23, John 3:16, 1 Corinthians 13:3-4, Ephesians 2:8-9, Romans 10:9-10, 1 Peter 2:2-3

The Hand

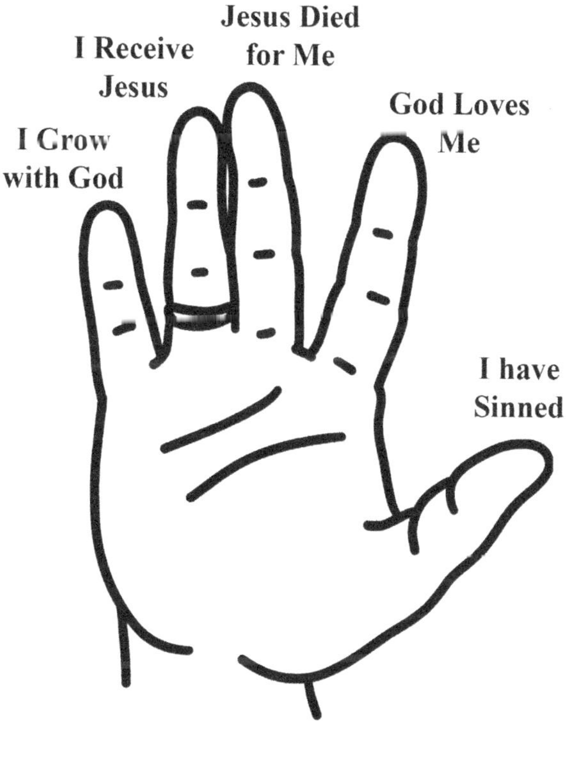

Source: Unknown

WHAT TO SAY:

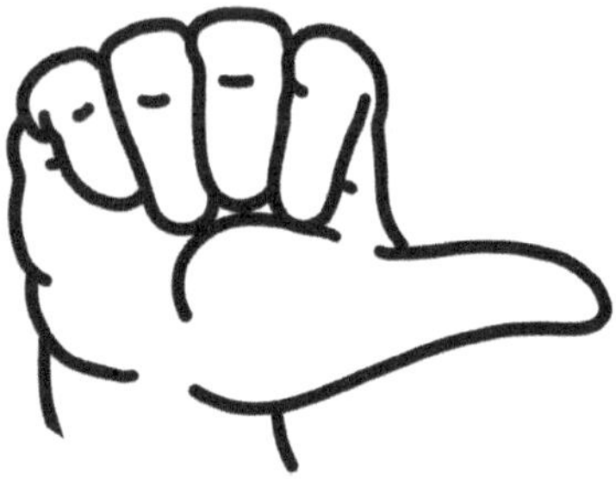

1. I Have Sinned. *"For all have sinned, and come short of the glory of God"* (Romans 3:23).

Action: Point to yourself with your thumbs.

The Bible says that everyone has sinned. Do you know what sin is? Sin is when we disobey God. Have you ever disobeyed your parents? Have you ever lied or stolen? All of these things are sins, and God hates sin.

2. God Loves Me. *"For God so loved the world that He gave His one and only Son, that whoever believes in Him shall not perish but have eternal life"* (John 3:16 NIV).

Action: Use your pointing finger to point to God.

God does hate sin, but God loves you and me. God loves us so much that He sent His only son, Jesus Christ, down to earth so that our sins can be forgiven.

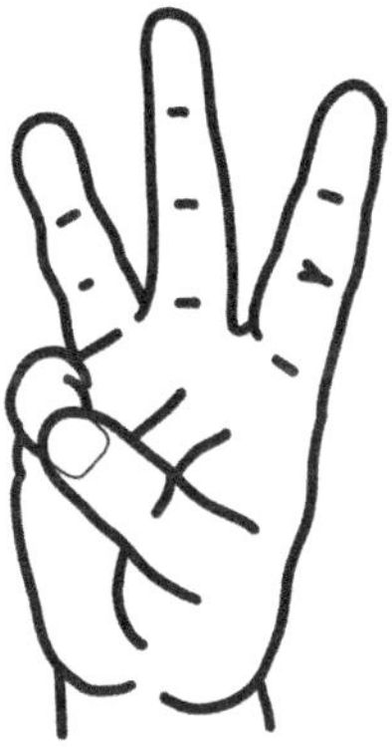

3. Jesus Died for Me. *"... How that Christ died for our sins according to the Scriptures; and that he was buried, and that he rose again the third day according to the scriptures"* (I Corinthians 13:3-4).

Action: When you hold your three middle fingers up, the middle one reminds you of how Jesus died on a cross between two other crosses.

The price for sin is death, so Jesus died on the cross to pay the price for all the wrong things that we have done. He died on a cross between two thieves. The thieves were being punished because they did something wrong, but Jesus never did anything wrong. Jesus was punished on the cross so that we would not have to be punished. But Jesus did not stay on the cross. After three days, Jesus rose from the dead, and today, He is alive.

4. I Receive Jesus. *"For by grace are we saved through faith; and not of yourselves: it is the gift of God. Not of works, lest any man should boast"* (Ephesians 2:8-9). *"...If you confess with your mouth the Lord Jesus, and shalt believe in thine heart that God raised him from the dead, thou shalt be saved. For with the heart, man believeth unto righteousness; and with the mouth confession is made unto salvation"* (Romans 10:9 10).

Action: Point to your ring finger and say, "I receive Jesus."

When a person gets married, they put a ring on this fourth finger to symbolize their love for their new spouse. The ring is a sign that they have chosen to marry the person that they love. In the same way, you can choose to follow Jesus.

Repeat this prayer after me: "Father, in the name of Jesus, I say with my mouth and believe in my heart that Jesus is Your Son. He died on the cross for my sins, and He came back to life again, and now He lives with You in heaven. Thank You, Father, for saving me. I make Jesus the Lord of my life. Amen."

5. I Grow with God

"Like newborn babies, crave pure spiritual milk, so that by it you may grow up in your salvation, now that you have tasted that the Lord is good" (1 Peter 2:2-3 NIV).

Action: Hold up your pinky finger.

This finger represents a new Christian. You may be small in size, but you can grow in God by listening to His word and spending time every day praying to God.

Thoughts about the Hand Illustration

- This is a simple five-step program that can be used to present the Gospel in a simple, easy-to-understand format. Your hand serves as an object lesson that you carry with you everywhere you go. It is especially effective at teaching children how to remember and share the Gospel. As I share the Gospel with children, I ask them to do the actions and to repeat the points. By the time I have reviewed the main points with the children several times, they have memorized the message and can share it with their friends.

CHAPTER 11

THE TEN COMMANDMENTS

Key Scriptures: Exodus 20:2-17

The Ten Commandments

Source: Ray Comfort is a street evangelist who witnesses primarily by using the Ten Commandments to prove that people are sinners.[16] His TV program *Way of the Master* has influenced thousands of people in their style of witnessing. Many churches use his *School of Biblical Evangelism* to train evangelism teams.

WHAT TO SAY:[17]

Would you consider yourself to be a good person? *Almost everyone answers with a "yes" because according to Proverbs 20:6, "Every man will declare his own goodness."*

I'm going to ask you a few questions to see if that's true.

How many lies have you told? Have you ever told a lie, even a small white one? What do you call someone who tells a lie? *Answer: A liar*

Have you ever stolen something, even if it was something small like a pen or a pencil? What do you call someone who steals? *Answer: A thief*

Have you ever used God's name in vain? That means using God's name to express disgust instead of a four-letter cuss word. Using God's name as a cuss word is called blasphemy and the Bible says, "God will not hold him guiltless whoever takes the Lord's name in vain" (Exodus 20:7).

Jesus said that if you look upon a person and lust after them, then

---

16 Ray Comfort, *"Are You a Good Person?"*, Accessed February 3, 2023, https://www.living-waters.com/are-you-a-good-person/?

17 Read several examples of how Ray Comfort witnesses in: Ray Comfort, *So Many Lions, So Few Daniels,* (Baker Books, Grand Rapids, MI, 2023). .

you have committed adultery in your heart (Matthew 5:28). Have you ever looked at a woman or a man with lust?

Have you ever hated your brother? According to 1 John 3:15, if you hate your brother, you are a murderer.

Talk About Judgment[18]

I'm not judging you but you've just admitted that you are a liar, a thief, a blasphemer, and an adulterer at heart and that's after looking at just a few of the 10 Commandments. You say you are a good person when it's clear you are not. If God were to judge you based on the 10 Commandments, would you be innocent or guilty?

Remember James 2:10 says, *"For whoever shall keep the whole Law, and yet offend in one point, he is guilty of all."*

If they say they would be innocent, then take them back to the commandments. "But you just told me that you've lied and stolen, and are guilty of committing adultery in your heart, etc."

Some people may say that they no longer do those things, in that case share with them the courtroom illustration:

If you were standing in front of a judge and you were guilty of a crime, like drug-dealing, can you tell the judge to let you go because it's been a long time since you've done your last drug deal? The answer is no. The same thing is true with with God, He is a holy and just God. Do you think God should let murders and thieves off the hook even if it has been a long time since they last murdered or stole?

18 Ray Comfort, *God Has a Wonderful Plan for Your Life: The Myth of the Modern Message*, (Bellflower, CA: Living Waters Publications, 2010), 91-93.

If they say that God is forgiving, then ask them, "Based on what will God forgive you?" *If they give you any answer other than "because Jesus Christ died on the cross for me" then bring their answer back to the courtroom illustration.*

Would you go to heaven or hell?

If God had to ask you "Why should I let you into My heaven?", what would your answer be?

They may reply with:

- *I am a good person.*
- *I go to church every Sunday.*
- *I am active in my community.*
- *I am a law-abiding citizen.*
- *I was raised in a Christian household.*

The truth is that none of the above will save you!

If they say heaven, then ask them, "How do you figure that?"

Continue to give the law to the person until the law has humbled them. It's only that once a sinner realizes that he/she is on their way to hell, then they are ready for grace (Jesus).

If they answer "hell", then ask them, "Does that concern you that if you were to die today that you would be on your way to hell?"

If yes, then give them the gospel.

If no, then ask them why not.

The Parachute Illustration[19]

Imagine you are sitting on a plane. Suddenly, the pilot makes an announcement. He says, "This plane is about to crash. Under your seat, there is a parachute. Please put it on immediately and get ready to jump out of the plane."

You have a choice. Do you choose to believe the pilot or do you choose to do nothing? The news about the plane crashing is bad news, but the news that there is a way to be saved is very good news.

Today, I have some bad news for you. Without Jesus, you will suffer eternal death and be separated from God forever. This is because of the Law of Sin. When you break God's law, you deserve to suffer the consequences of breaking His law. The Law of Gravity will make you fall from a plane and the Law of Sin will cause you to be eternally separated from God.

However, I also have some good news for you. There is a way for you to be saved. There is a parachute that can save your life. His name is Jesus, but you must trust Him for salvation. If you do not put on your parachute, you will surely die.

Some people try to save themselves through their own efforts. This is like jumping out of a plane and trying to fly by flapping your arms. You cannot save yourself, but you can be saved if you trust in Jesus.

When you put on a parachute, you can be saved from falling. In the same way, you must "put on the Lord Jesus Christ" and He will save you from sin.

19 Ray Comfort, *God Has a Wonderful Plan for Your Life: The Myth of the Modern Message*, (Bellflower, CA: Living Waters Publications, 2010), 69.

Talk About the Gospel

Imagine you were in a courtroom facing judgment for a crime that you committed. Let's say it was for stealing money. You were about to receive the punishment that you deserved by being sent to jail when suddenly, someone comes along and pays your fine. That's what Jesus did for you.

Jesus paid the fine for your sins. Jesus came in the flesh, died for your sins on the cross, and rose from the dead. He will give eternal life to all those who believe in Him. To receive eternal life all you have to do is:

1. Put your trust in Jesus the same way that you would in a parachute when jumping from a plane. That parachute is going to save your life when you jump from the plane. Likewise, you are trusting that Jesus will save your life when you go into eternity.

2. Repent of your sins. To repent means to make a U-turn or to change your mind. So, abandon your sins and turn toward God.

Thoughts about the Ten Commandments

1. I am including this script for witnessing in this book because it is popular among street preachers even though I think that this method of preaching often comes across as harsh. Using the Ten Commandments as a witnessing tool has been made popular by Ray Comfort, an evangelist from New Zealand, who now lives in California and has produced many videos demonstrating his methods of witnessing. Over 600 million people have viewed his videos on YouTube. I have great respect for Ray Comfort as a

brother in the Lord, although I do have some critiques of the method he uses.

3. Ray Comfort often quotes Psalm 19:7, *"The Law of the Lord is perfect, converting the soul."* He argues it is God's law that brings the knowledge of sin. He uses the Ten Commandments to remind people of the law of God that is written on our hearts and to spark the conscience. At first, everyone claims to be a good person, but when our actions are held up against God's perfect Law, it quickly becomes evident that we are not perfect. Then Comfort warns his listeners of the judgment which is to come.

4. Ray Comfort does not give altar calls or lead people in a prayer of salvation.[20] In large part, this is because his theology is rooted in Calvinism and most Calvinists disagree that a person can choose to accept Christ, instead they emphasize that God chooses those whom He wills to be saved.

4. If Ray Comfort was a car salesman…

Is Ray Comfort's style of evangelism the best way to reach people with the Gospel? I think the best way to answer this question is to take his script and put it in the context of trying to sell a car.

A man is driving around in his car and is approached by Ray Comfort, a car salesman.

Ray: Excuse me, sir, is this your car?

Man: Yes, it is.

---

20 Ray Comfort, *Hell's Best Kept Secret,* (Springdale, PA: Whitaker House, 1989), 66-67.

Ray: Would you consider your car to be a good car?

Man: I suppose so. It's not perfect but it gets me around.

Ray: Do you mind if I give you a test to see how good your car is?

Man: Sure, why not.

Ray: Does your car get good gas mileage? Before you answer, keep in mind that the US government defines good gas mileage as any car that gets better than 40 miles per gallon.

Man: Well, I get about 27 MPG, so I guess by your definition, I don't get good gas mileage.

Ray: Does your air conditioning work?

Man: No, it gave out a few months ago. I need to refill my Freon. In the meantime, I just roll down the windows.

Ray: So, what does that make your car?

Man: Hot, I guess.

Ray: Call it what it is. Your car is uncomfortable, burning, scorching, sweltering, and you sweat when you are driving around.

Man: OK…

Ray: One more question. Has your car ever been in an accident? Is your car dented?

Man: No, I've never been in an accident.

Ray: What about the scratch along the side of your door?

Man: I forgot about that. Someone ran a shopping cart into my car at the grocery store.

Ray: I thought you said you had never been in an accident. Wouldn't you call a shopping cart scratch an accident?

Man: Sure, but it's not that big a deal.

Ray: It is a big deal. That scratch can knock hundreds of dollars off of the value of your car. So, let's get this straight. By your own admission, your car is uncomfortable, damaged, and does not get good gas mileage. Admit it. You have a bad car.

Man: OK, I admit it. I should get a new car.

Ray: I want you to think about that. See you later.

The man drives away scratching his head, feeling bad about his car, but HE DOES NOT KNOW HOW TO BUY A NEW ONE.

What use is a salesman who never closes the deal? An evangelist needs to close the deal.

What salesman convinces the customer he needs a new car without giving him the opportunity to actually purchase a new car? No new car salesman would ever try to sell his cars with this sales technique. Instead of focusing on the flaws in the customer's current car, most salesmen highlight the benefits of their new product. Most salesmen understand that you catch more flies with honey than with vinegar.

The problem with Ray Comfort's style of evangelism is that he never brings people to a point where they can decide to follow Jesus.

He makes them feel bad about sin but never tells them that Jesus can wash away sin. On his TV program, Ray Comfort never leads anyone in a salvation prayer. In his book *Hell's Best Kept Secret,* he actually condemns the use of altar calls.

- It is better to focus on Jesus rather than on the Ten Commandments. Paul called the Ten Commandments "a ministry of death and condemnation" (2 Corinthians 3:7). Ray Comfort preaches bad news, but fails to preach the Gospel, which is "good news." Although to be fair, he would contest this point by using his illustration about a person in a crashing plane who is asked to put in a parachute. Before the person thinks it is a good idea to put on an uncomfortable parachute, he must be convinced of the bad news that the plane is going to crash.

- Bill Bright taught people to start witnessing by saying, "God loves you and has a wonderful plan for your life." Ray Comfort feels this approach to witnessing is a huge mistake.[21]

- However, I believe it is easier to draw people to God by talking about the goodness of God instead of the sinfulness of humankind. The best way to witness is to reveal Jesus. Jesus said, *"If I be lifted up, I will draw all men unto me"* (John 12:32). When Jesus met the Samaritan woman at the well, He revealed Himself to the woman (John 4:26). The more people know about Jesus, the more likely they will be to live for God.

People are far more likely to come to God if they discover that Jesus came to give them *"abundant life"* (John 10:10).[22] Paul explained

21 Ray Comfort, *God Has a Wonderful Plan for Your Life: The Myth of the Modern Message,* (Bellflower, CA: Living Waters Publications, 2010).

22 Listen to a discussion I had with Ray Comfort about John 10:10 on The Evangelism Podcast, https://kingministries.com/the-evangelism-podcast-with-daniel-king/

that it is *"the goodness of God that draws all men to repentance"* (Romans 2:4). When witnessing, it is better to talk about how good God is than it is to condemn people for their sins.

The Jewish Pharisees knew the Ten Commandments forwards and backward, yet they still failed to live perfect lives. Knowing the Ten Commandments never gave anyone the ability to live a holy life. The only way for us to become righteous is through the work Jesus did on the cross. Acts 2:21 says, *"Everyone who calls on the name of Jesus shall be saved."*

When witnessing, tell people how good Jesus is and give them a chance to cry out to Jesus. Trust the Holy Spirit to do the work of conversion in their hearts. Don't condemn people by screaming about how bad they are. Instead, lift people up by telling them how good Jesus is.

- The name of Ray Comfort's ministry is The Way of the Master. In the Bible, wasn't it the Way of the Master to cast out demons and heal the sick? I have never seen Ray Comfort do either of these things while he is witnessing.

| CHAPTER 12 |

THE LENGTH OF ETERNITY

Key Verses: Philippians 3:13-14 "*...One thing I do, forgetting those things which are behind and reaching forward to those things which are ahead, I press toward the goal for the prize of the upward call of God in Christ Jesus*" (NKJV).

The Length of Eternity

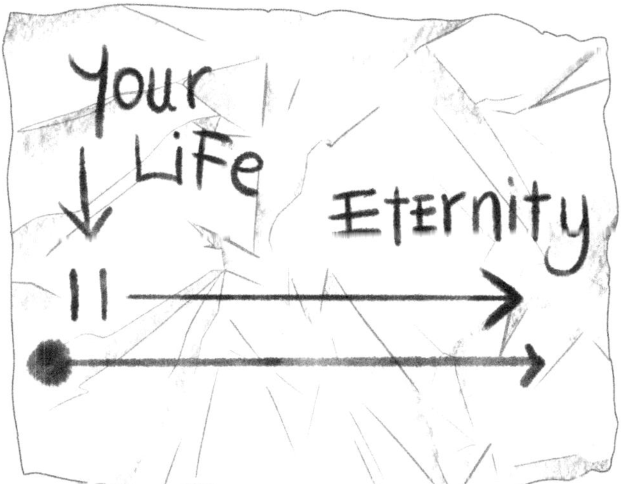

Source: Francis Chan[23]

23 Francis Chan, "Stunning Illustration of Eternity," (Accessed November 2, 2019), https://

WHAT TO SAY:

Imagine that this line is a timeline of your existence that goes on forever. The line never stops. How long is eternity? It keeps going forever and it never stops.

Draw a line with an arrow pointing off into the distance.

Here is your birth.

Draw a dot representing the beginning of your life.

Do you see this short part? This small section of the line represents your time here on earth. You are born, you live, and you die.

Draw two lines representing birth and death.

Have you ever seen a gravestone? They often feature the date of birth and the date of death. In between those two dates is a short hyphen. The length of that hyphen represents how fleetingly short life is.

---

www.youtube.com/watch?v=YWk7RUg3ZV4

After you die, you have all of eternity somewhere else. Some people are obsessed with this short part. It is all they think about. They plan to work hard so that they can enjoy a few short years here on earth.

However, what about the rest of eternity? The Bible teaches that what I do during this short time period will determine what happens to me for the rest of eternity.

Imagine your life. You are born, you live, and you die. Now imagine how long eternity is.

Write the word "eternity."

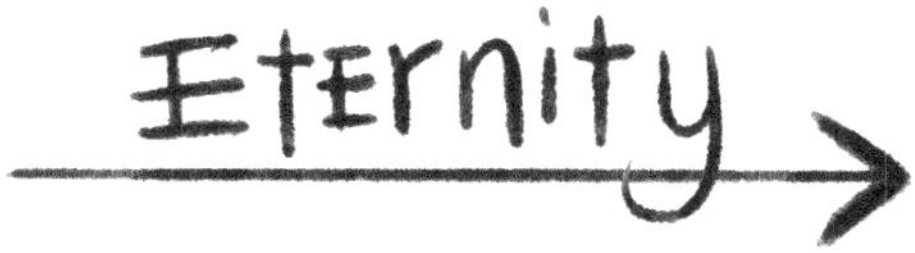

Why would I spend the little time that I have here trying to make myself as comfortable as possible and enjoying myself as much as I can while I forget about the rest of eternity?

When I face God, I do not get another chance. I have one chance to get the rest of eternity right. Our time on earth can end at any second for anyone. We have one chance at this life and then comes eternity.

So, the question I want to ask you today is: Are you ready for eternity?

Thoughts about the Length of Eternity Illustration

- This picture is a good way to bring up the length of eternity. Thinking about this can easily lead to a discussion of Pascal's Wager.

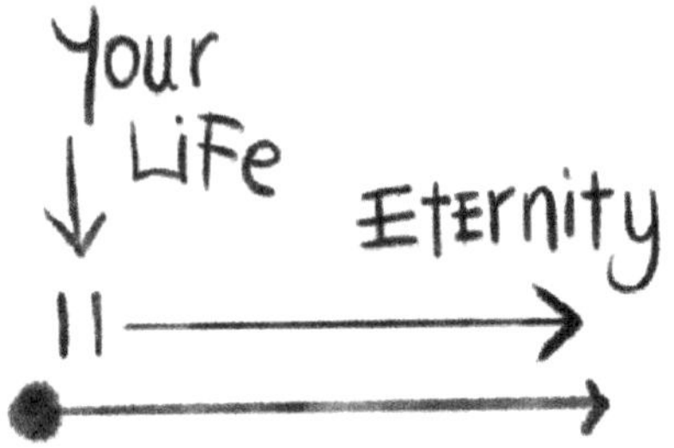

Blaise Pascal (1623-1662) was an intellectual giant, and his inquisitive mind delved into many different disciplines. At the age of thirty-one, Pascal had a supernatural conversion experience. After his salvation experience, Pascal wrote his *Pensées*, a series of thoughts about God and philosophy that were gathered up and published after his death. In this work, Pascal proposed the idea that is known as "Pascal's Wager." Because of his gambling days and his work on probability theory, Pascal was deeply interested in making bets. In the wager, he bets that it makes more sense to be a Christian than it does to be an atheist. The elements of his bet are as follows:

Premise A: God may or may not be real.

Premise B: If God is real and the Bible is true, then I risk an eternity of life and happiness if I do not serve Him. (More than that I also risk an eternity of infinite misery in hell.)

Premise C: If God is not real and I live as if He is, I only lose a finite amount of happiness here on this earth.

Conclusion: Therefore, since the infinities of heaven and happiness and of hell and torment outweigh the finite-

> ness of life on earth, I will wager that there is a God, and live my life accordingly.[24]

I like what Christian Hip Hop artist, Lecrae, observed, "If I'm wrong about God, I wasted my life. If you are wrong about God, you wasted your eternity."

---

24 Lee C Archie, "Blaise Pascal, 'Pascal's Wager,'" *Philosophy of Religion* http://philosophy.lander.edu/intro/pascal.shtml#Reconstruct (June 26, 2006)

CHAPTER 13

THE FOUR POINTS GOSPEL

Key Verses: 1 John 3:16, 1 John 4:16, Psalm 139:13, Romans 8:38-39, Romans 5:12, Romans 3:23, James 2:10, Isaiah 59:2, Romans 6:23, 2 Peter 3:9, Isaiah 53:6, Hebrews 12:2, John 3:16-18, Romans 10:9-10, Deuteronomy 30:19-20

The Four Points Gospel

Source: The 4 Points[25]

25 "The Four Points", Accessed February 3, 2023, https://www.the4points.com

WHAT TO SAY:

1. God Loves Me

If you're a member of the human race, then God loves you; not just with any old 'love' but with a love that will last forever (Jeremiah 31:3) and one which drove Him to give His own son, Jesus, to die in your place. As it says in 1 John 3:16, *"This is how we know what love is: Jesus Christ laid down his life for us."*

You see, love is not just something that God does, it's what He is. He defines the true meaning of love. In 1 John 4:16, it simply says, *"God is love"*.

Why would God love us? Why would He love you? If you have ever had a child, then you may be able to understand something of how God feels towards you. When my wife was pregnant with our first child, I had a photo from the ultrasound scan which I was so proud of. I loved that baby so much. I had never before experienced the force of love like this.

Why? He didn't really look like much. He couldn't do anything to impress me or say anything to please me. He was just a white smudge on a black square. I didn't love my son because he deserved it, I loved him because he was MY SON! In a mysterious way, my wife and I had 'made' him. He was ours.

Whether you believe it or not, God created you. In Psalm 139:13

it says, *"For you created my inmost being; you knit me together in my mother's womb."*

You are the work of His hands, His own creation, and nothing you or anyone else may do can change that fact or His love for you. Romans 8:38-39 says *"...neither death nor life, neither angels nor demons, neither the present nor the future, nor any powers, neither height nor depth, nor anything else in all creation, will be able to separate us from the love of God..."*

You may wonder how there can be a loving God when there is so much sadness & evil in the world. The simplest answer to that is that God created us to have free will rather than running the world and us like robots. Much of the sadness in the world is due to mankind's wrong decisions and selfish actions. Ultimately the Bible teaches that evil, sickness & death only entered the world because of a wrong choice, the disobedience of the first man, Adam. Romans 5:12 says *"...sin entered the world through one man, and death through sin, and in this way death came to all men..."*

The ultimate demonstration and proof of God's love for you is the death of Jesus on the cross over 2000 years ago, but we'll come on to that in point number 3.

2. I Have Sinned

Romans 3:23 says, *"all have sinned and fall short of the glory of God."* That means that every human being has failed to meet the perfect standard of God's goodness and righteousness. We have failed because we have done things our way, not God's way. We have disobeyed His instruction which He wrote in both the Bible and in our consciences. God's law is like a pane of glass; it's either broken or it isn't. It's no good saying "I only lied; I never stole".

James 2:10 says, *"For whoever keeps the whole law and yet stumbles at just one point is guilty of breaking all of it."* Whether it's murder or whether it's just a 'white' lie, whether it's adultery or just jealousy, every sin keeps us from meeting God's standard and has both consequences and penalties!

The consequences of sin can be numerous. If we lie, we can be caught and break relationships & trust. If we steal, we can be caught and prosecuted. Yet the most serious consequence of sin is that it separates us from God and from the relationship He created us to have with Him. Isaiah 59:2 says, *"But your iniquities have separated you from your God; your sins have hidden His face from you, so that He will not hear."* Have you ever wondered why God feels so far away?

Even more serious is the penalty for sin. Romans 6:23 says, *"For the wages of sin is death,"* i.e. death is what you earn from sinning. Not physical death, since that is inevitable for all of us. It's the ultimate statistic: 1 out of 1 die. The Bible is referring to spiritual death, that is, the assumption that we are more than just physical bodies; that we have a spirit or soul which persists after our bodies die. It is unclear exactly what it means for us to face spiritual death, but it is clear that it is the opposite of God's desired plan for you and me, which is that our spirit goes to dwell with Him forever in His presence. This is what the Bible calls heaven.

So, we all have a big problem. We have all sinned, and because God is perfectly just, this sin means we must all face spiritual death and eternal separation from God. This is what the Bible calls Hell!

If you're unhappy about this, you'll be pleased to know that because of His great love for you, God was even more unhappy with the situation (2 Peter 3:9).

3. Jesus Died for Me

The just penalty for our sin, the wrong things every one of us has done, is spiritual death - separation from God. In the Old Testament times, God allowed animals to be sacrificed for sin and would accept the shed blood as a substitute for the people's own life. But ever since man had first sinned, God had planned a permanent solution; the ultimate sacrifice that could pay the punishment for everyone's sin and see justice done.

The plan was this: to send his own son, Jesus, who was Himself God, to be born as a human baby and live on this earth, leading a perfect, sinless life, and when He had done this, to voluntarily offer His own life as a sacrifice to pay the penalty for our sin. He would experience not just death, but separation from God, the only time Jesus had ever been completely separated from His father.

This was prophesied hundreds of years before Jesus' birth by Isaiah 53:6: *"We're all like sheep who've wandered off and gotten lost. We've all done our own thing, gone our own way."* God has piled all our sins, everything we've done wrong, on Jesus.

The fact that Jesus lived and walked on this earth is historically undeniable. There is more evidence of the existence of Jesus than there is of Julius Caesar. He was born in Bethlehem, grew up as a carpenter, and lived a perfect life, never sinning once. He loved & healed people, taught them about God, and was then falsely accused and crucified by the Romans outside of Jerusalem. He did all of this willingly because He loved you so much that He wanted to save you from the judgment that you deserve.

Hebrews 12:2 says, *"...for the joy set before Him [Jesus] endured the cross, scorning its shame"."* Then, Jesus came back to life again after 3 days in 'hell' since death could not hold the Son of God.

This wonderful plan is summed up in one of the most well know Bible verses, John 3:16-18: *"This is how much God loved the world: He gave his Son, His one and only Son. And this is why: so that no one need be destroyed; by believing in him, anyone can have a whole and lasting life. God didn't go to all the trouble of sending His Son merely to point an accusing finger, telling the world how bad it was. He came to help, to put the world right again. Anyone who trusts in Him is acquitted; anyone who refuses to trust Him has long since been under the death sentence without knowing it. And why? Because of that person's failure to believe in the one-of-a-kind Son of God when introduced to Him"* (The Message Bible).

You might think that's the end of the matter but there's one more all-important point that makes the difference between life & death.

4. I Need to Decide

God has done His part. Jesus gave His own life as a punishment for OUR sin. We didn't deserve it. It wasn't 'fair', but that's how much God loves you.

Now you have to decide if you want to accept this gift of forgiveness and this promise of eternal life. If you want to be free from the punishment that you brought on yourself by not doing things God's way, you need to decide to surrender to God and do things His way from now on. You need to believe that He exists, that He loves you, and that He died for you.

Romans 10:9-10 says, *"...if you confess with your mouth, "Jesus is Lord," and believe in your heart that God raised him from the dead, you will be saved."*

The choice is yours. You still have free will, just the way God created you. You can surrender your life to God, the creator of the universe, who loves you more than anyone else ever will and only wants the best for you, or, you can walk away and face the inevitable consequences. Deuteronomy 30:19-20 sums it up like this: *"This day I call heaven and earth as witnesses against you that I have set before you life and death, blessings and curses. Now choose life, so that you and your children may live and that you may love the LORD your God, listen to His voice, and hold fast to Him."*

If you want to know this forgiveness and know this God who created you for a relationship with Him; if you want to have that separation between you and God removed and have the punishment and guilt of all the wrong things you've ever done wiped away, then you can, right now! Just say this prayer, and if you are sincere, God will see your heart and save you.

"Dear God, thank you that You died for me and want the best for me in every situation. I'm sorry for ignoring You and doing things my way. I realize now that my sin has hurt You and the people around me, and for this, I am truly sorry. Thank you, Jesus, that You came and took the punishment for my sin. Thank you for giving Your life for me. Please forgive me and help me now as I decide to live only for You. Amen"

Thoughts About the Four Points Gospel

- The symbol is cryptic and difficult to understand until you know its meaning. This helps create the intended response and opportunities to share your faith as people ask you the meaning.

- The logo looks like an equation i.e. heart times cross is what? This also helps to generate intrigue and provoke a question that allows you to share the Gospel.

- These four pictures are an excellent way to remember and communicate the Gospel.

- The Four Points Gospel is similar to the Four Spiritual Laws which was taught by Bill Bright from Campus Crusade for Christ. The order in how the Gospel is presented is the same, but the Four Points Gospel is more concise and is updated for a contemporary audience. The minimalistic style of the symbols is attractive, and the shorter presentation is ideal for today's fast-paced, post-Christian world.

CHAPTER 14

F.A.I.T.H.

Key Scriptures: Ephesians 1:7a, John 3:16, Matthew 7:21a, James 2:13, Romans 3:23, Luke 13:3, Romans 10:9, John 10:10, John 10:3

F.A.I.T.H

Source: J.D. Greear and Rob Turner[26]

26 Greear, J.D. and Rob Turner, Derwin Gray, Ben Reed, *Engage: A Practical Guide to Evangelism,* (Nashville, TN: Lifeway Press, 2013), 76.

WHAT TO SAY:

What is the key to being saved? It is the word "FAITH." Here is an easy way to remember the important components of the Gospel using the acronym F.A.I.T.H.

F is for FORGIVENESS.

In order to receive eternal life and go to heaven, we must receive God's forgiveness. Our sin and disobedience separate us from God and cause us to deserve eternal punishment. However, God's love and mercy are so great that He offers us the opportunity for forgiveness through faith in Jesus Christ and His sacrifice on the cross. When we confess our sins and ask for forgiveness, God forgives us and cleanses us from all unrighteousness, making us righteous in His eyes. This newfound relationship with God through forgiveness grants us the gift of eternal life and a place in heaven, where we will be with Him forever. Without forgiveness, we would remain separated from God and condemned to an eternity apart from Him. It is essential that we receive God's forgiveness in order to have a right relationship with Him and attain eternal life in heaven.

Ephesians 1:7a "*In Him we have redemption through His blood, the forgiveness of sins...*"

A

A is for AVAILABLE.

God's forgiveness is available for everyone who asks for it. Regardless of the magnitude or frequency of one's sin, God is ready and willing to forgive. Jesus says in Mark 11:24, *"Therefore I tell you, whatever you ask for in prayer, believe that you have received it, and it will be yours."* This means that as long as we approach God with a sincere heart, confessing our sins and asking for His forgiveness, He will grant it to us. The apostle John wrote in 1 John 1:9, *"If we confess our sins, he is faithful and just and will forgive us our sins and purify us from all unrighteousness."* God's love and mercy are boundless, and He desires to have a relationship with every person. By asking for His forgiveness, we open the door to this relationship and experience the forgiveness, peace, and hope that only He can provide. No one is beyond the reach of God's forgiveness, and it is available to all who seek it through faith in Jesus Christ.

John 3:16 *"For God so loved the world that He gave His only begotten Son, that whoever believes in Him should not perish but have everlasting life"*

However, forgiveness does not happen automatically. Matthew 7:21 says, *"Not everyone who says to Me, 'Lord, Lord,' shall enter the kingdom of heaven…"*

I is for IMPOSSIBLE.

It is impossible for God to allow sin into heaven. Since God is just and holy, He must judge sin. It is impossible for God to allow sin into heaven due to His nature as a just and holy God. As the source of all goodness and perfection, God cannot tolerate anything that goes against His moral character. Since sin is inherently evil and against God's will, He must judge it. James 2:13 tells us, *"For judgment is without mercy to the one who has shown no mercy. Mercy triumphs over judgment"* (NKJV).

The truth is that everyone has sinned. All individuals, regardless of their actions or intentions, have sinned at some point in their lives and therefore fall short of God's standard of holiness. This means that without a solution for sin, all people would be separated from God and excluded from heaven. Romans 3:23 says, *"for all have sinned and fall short of the glory of God…"*

T is for TURN.

The word turn means to repent from a sinful life. Turning away from sin and towards God means recognizing that our actions and choices have separated us from God and His perfect will for our lives. By acknowledging our sin and seeking forgiveness, we demonstrate our humility and commitment to living a life that is pleasing to God. Turning towards God requires a change of heart and a willingness to follow Him, which is facilitated by developing a closer relationship with Him through prayer, reading the Bible, and being active in a church community. This transformation of heart and mind is called repentance, and it leads to a changed life as we seek to align our actions and thoughts with God's will. Turning away from sin and towards God is not a one-time event but a continuous process as we continue to grow in our faith and strive to live in obedience to Him. It is through this process that we can experience the fullness of God's grace, love, and forgiveness in our lives. Luke 13:3 says, *"unless you repent you will all likewise perish"*

In order to be saved, we have to turn away from our sin and turn towards Christ. Romans 10:9 reads, *"if you confess with your mouth the Lord Jesus and believe in your heart that God has raised Him from the dead, you will be saved"*

H

H is for HEAVEN.

Heaven is where those who are saved will live for all of eternity. Heaven is a place of perfect peace, joy, and love where God dwells and where the faithful will spend eternity. It is a place of unending beauty and bliss where there will be no more pain, suffering, or death. God wants all people to go to heaven, and it is His ultimate desire that everyone will one day be reconciled to Him and experience the fullness of His love and presence. Through faith in Jesus Christ and a life lived in obedience to God, people can be assured of their place in heaven and experience the fullness of God's love and peace both now and forever.

John 10:10 reveals the contrast between the devil's plan for your life and God's plan for your life: *"The thief does not come except to steal, and to kill, and to destroy. I have come that they may have life, and that they may have it more abundantly."*

John 10:3 promises, *"To him the doorkeeper opens, and the sheep hear his voice; and he calls his own sheep by name and leads them out"*

So how can someone turn away from sin and receive forgiveness and the gift of eternal life? The secret is to trust Jesus Christ and to ask Him for forgiveness.

Thoughts About the F.A.I.T.H Illustration

- I like starting a conversation about God with the words "Forgiveness" and "Available" instead of starting with pointing a finger at humanity's sin. The F.A.I.T.H. acronym is a soft way of presenting the Good News without turning people off by shouting bad news at them.

CHAPTER 15

THE BIG STORY

Key Scriptures: Genesis 3, Ephesians 1:7, Galatians 1:4

The Big Story

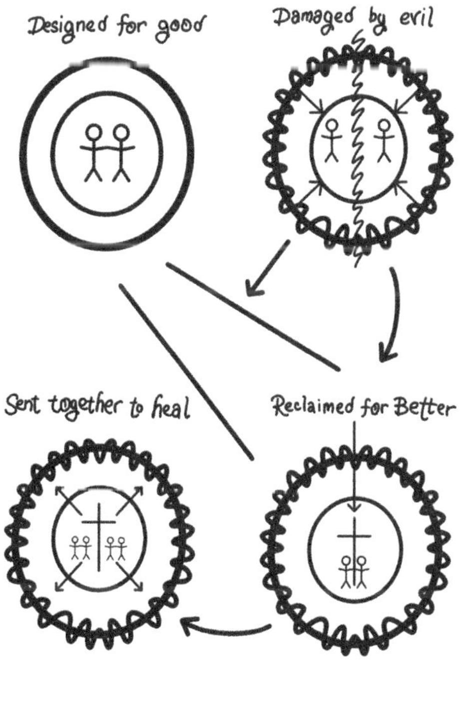

Source: James Choung,[27] this illustration is used by Intervarsity[28] and Cru

WHAT TO SAY:

Introduction: The Ache

Would you like to hear the core message Jesus came to teach or the basic message of the Bible? What's our world like? What do you see on the news?

• *Draw the world (outer circle) and the people within in, slightly apart.*

Would we agree that the world is messed up?

• *Draw a squiggly line over the outer circle to represent a world in damage and shock.*

27 James Choung, 'The Big Story: A Gospel Presentation" (July 2017). Accessed August 15, 2020, http://www.jameschoung.net/big-story-training.pdf

28 Intervarsity, "The Evangelism Toolkit, the Big Story, (Accessed February 3, 2023), https://2100.intervarsity.org/overview/big-story

The world is messed up; that's obvious. But what's more interesting is the human response: how do you feel about this kind of world? No normal person thinks that suffering, violence, and oppression are good things. No one throws a party for the bloodbath in Darfur, when a child is infected with AIDS, or when the Towers fell in New York. So, what does this mean? Most people ache for a better world. However, our universal ache speaks of something more. Just like hunger points to food and thirst points to water, our universal ache for a better world means that such a world either once existed or will one day exist.

Part 1: Designed for Good

In the Christian worldview, God created a good and wonderful world where, in the beginning, everything was right.

• *Draw a new circle in the top left corner representing the world. Draw people, who are not necessarily Adam and Eve, close together to represent intimacy and community.*

On a bigger level, creation was designed to take care of us, and we were designed to take care of creation. We were made to be interdependent on each other.

On a relational level, people were designed to take care of each other. They were made to be in true community, with the freedom to love and be loved, to serve and be served, and to be themselves without shame in front of each other.

Lastly, on a personal level, we were each designed to be in a relationship with the God who created us, one full of love and intimacy. God hung out with us and we liked being with Him. We were meant to love and serve each other as well.

• *Draw the inner circle to represent God's presence with us.*

The world and all that is in it were designed for good.

• *Write the words "Designed for good" at the top.*

But what happened to this good world? How did we get to where we are today?

Part 2: Damaged by Evil

When God was in charge, we had a wonderful world. However, we wanted to be in charge so that all of creation and everyone in it could be used for our own benefit instead of its intended design and purpose of serving each other. Instead, it became all about us.

• *Draw the arrows that point inward to the people that represent self-centeredness.*

On the bigger level, we have damaged creation. We fill the air with pollutants so that we can have a comfortable lifestyle and it fights back with hurricanes and tsunamis. But there are also other larger issues such as racism, sexism, slavery, injustice, and oppression that all damage us and our world.

On a relational level, we damage each other, and others hurt us whether we mean to or not.

When we live for only ourselves, it's easy to take and gain without regard for other people.

• *Draw a squiggly line right down the middle, splitting the people from each other.*

On a personal level, we damage our souls and their relationships with God. We are afraid of God now, and in our fear, we try to ignore Him and live for ourselves. Yet we are only hurting ourselves, and we will never be the kind of people that we want and dream to be.

We and the world are damaged by evil. We're all damaged and are consistently contributing to the mess.

• *Write the words "Damaged by evil" in the top right.*

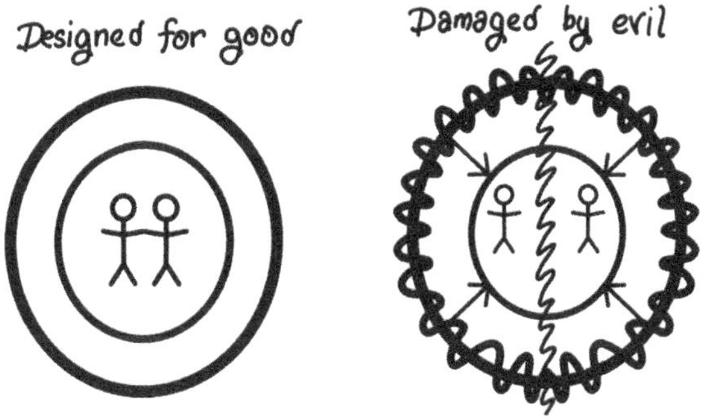

Where have you seen damage in your own life or the lives around you?

Part 3: Restored for better

God loved the world too much to leave it this way.

• *Draw the world (outer circle) again with the squiggly lines. Draw an arrow coming down from above into the world's mess and a cross in the center of the circle.*

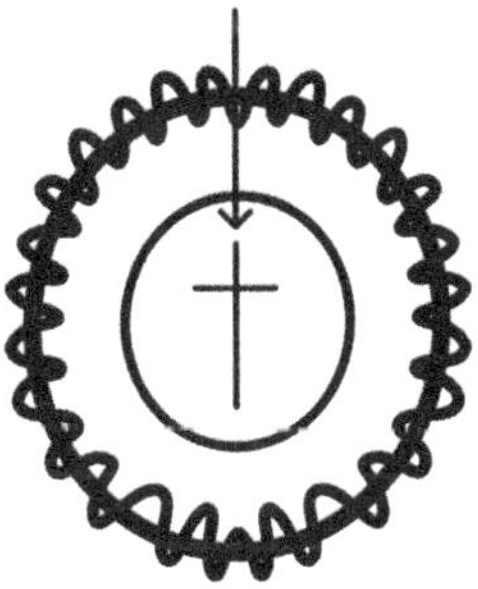

God came to the planet as Jesus 2,000 years ago and started a new thing: a resistance movement against evil, though not with military revolt or communal escapism. Instead, He taught us a better way to live and wants to give us the power to overcome evil in us and around us. Jesus took on all of the damage and died on the cross, letting it die with Him.

But He also came back to life, proving that evil doesn't have the final say. In the mystery of faith, we too die with Jesus to truly live in and with Him.

In so doing, everything, including us, is restored for the better. On an even bigger level, He restored creation so that all of it could be used in good ways. All of the world's systems, corporations, governments, schools, etc. have the new potential to usher in God's values of love, peace, and justice. Oppression and injustice can cease. He also restored our relationships so that we can love and forgive each other. Damaged relationships can be healed.

• *Put people at the foot of the cross learning to be like Jesus. Write "Reclaimed for better" at the top of this circle.*

Lastly, God restored our relationships with Himself. People don't have to live self-centered lives or be afraid of God anymore.

He forgives the ways we contribute to the damage in the world. Now we can truly live with God in a relationship full of love and intimacy.

The good news is that the revolution has begun and we're all invited. Jesus came to restore the world and everything in it for the better.

Part 4: Sent Together to Heal

Jesus wants us to join this resistance movement against evil and to go out and heal the world.

• *Draw the outer circle again (fourth circle), again with the squiggly lines because the fullness of the Kingdom of God has not yet arrived. Draw the cross in the center ag*ain. Draw the two pairs of people near the inner circle.

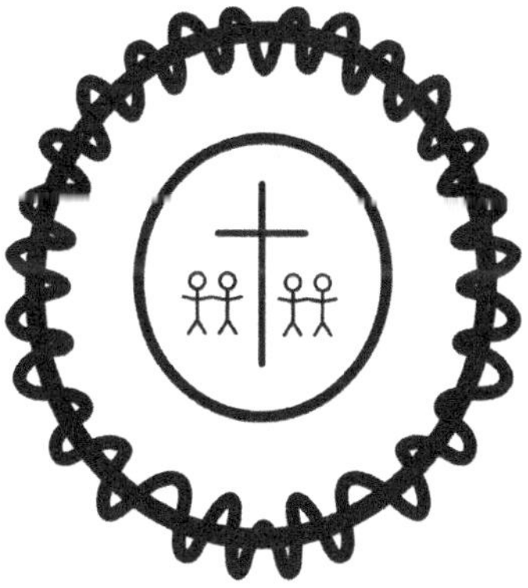

On a personal level, we're called to submit to Jesus' leadership and become more like Him. We need to become the kind of good that we want to see in the world. So, we admit our contribution to the damage, receive forgiveness, and trust Jesus, letting Him take charge of our lives instead.

As we're becoming more like Jesus, we're also called to heal relationships, our own and those of others. We ask for forgiveness and forgive others. When we do this, we're freed to love each other.

Lastly, on a bigger level, we're called to heal systems. We're called to protect the environment and fight injustice and oppression. It's overwhelming, but we're called to do it together.

• *Draw the arrows leading outward which represent God's Spirit. Write "Sent together to heal" at the top of this circle.*

Many Christians around us have gotten stuck in the third circle, not helping to heal the planet. But Jesus wanted His followers to be in this fourth circle by being sent together to heal.

We don't go alone, but rather with the power of God's Spirit and the community of God's people with us. He'll be with us. With these resources, Jesus is asking us to be sent together to heal the planet.

Response

We can't go straight to the last circle. We need to become the kind of good that we want to see in the world. In everything that we do, we bring all that we are to it: our motivations, our instincts, and our actions. We are all damaged, and we need healing before we can really heal what is around us. Jesus does that the best. By trusting Him and giving Him leadership over our lives, we can become the kind of good that we want to see around us.

• *Draw 2 parallel lines that block the path between the 2nd and 4th circles. Then draw 3 arrows: the 1st is unable to reach the other side. The other 2 show a path to the 4th circle only through Jesus.*

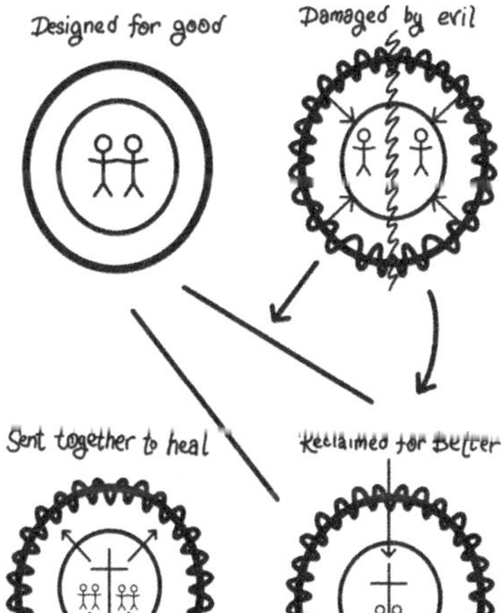

So, which one of these circles do you relate to? In the first, everything's fine. In the second, you're overwhelmed by the problems. In the third, you've made some commitment to Jesus but are holding back. In the fourth, you're in the movement of God with His people. Where are you?

• (If first circle): But we already said that the world needs help. What's your role in helping to heal the world?

• (If second circle): Tell me about it. Jesus is offering you a way to overcome it. Would you like to know how?

• (If third circle): That's a great start, but it's clear that Jesus is asking you for more. What's keeping you from joining His movement to heal the world?

• (If fourth circle): What you're doing is in line with the values of the Kingdom of God, but you could be doing so much more with God's presence and with His people. You could be a part of something that will last. Would you like to be a part of it? Would you like to let Jesus be the leader of your life and join His movement to heal the planet? Will you trust Him with your life?

Thoughts About the Big Story

- The Big Story Gospel presentation is another attempt to communicate the Gospel to a post-modern audience. The concept of sin is rarely worried about by millennials, the X generation, or the Y generation. Instead, young people are worried about global warming, terrorism, racism, gun violence, and tolerance of various lifestyles. This presentation will give you the opportunity to talk about how messed up the world is. Instead of focusing on personal sin, this presentation of the Gospel allows the presenter to deal with the sins of the whole world.

- In my experience, the Big Story is too complex It is hard to use this illustration because there are lots of moving parts, lots of drawing, and explaining and it can be confusing to both the speaker and the listener.

CHAPTER 16

JESUS AT THE DOOR

Key Scripture: Jesus said, "*Behold, I stand at the door and knock. If anyone hears my voice and opens the door, I will come in and eat with that person, and they with me*" (Revelation 3:20).

Jesus At the Door

Source: Jesus at the Door was written by Scott McNamara.[29]

29 Scott McNamara, "Evangelism Made Easy," Accessed February 3, 2023, https://jesusatthedoor.com/

WHAT TO SAY:

Start by showing the Jesus at the Door Picture.

Have you seen this picture before? Do you pray?

This is Jesus knocking at the door of your heart. The handle is on the inside; only you can let Him in.

Lots of people pray, but praying is like talking through a door. You know He's there somewhere, but you don't know Him personally.

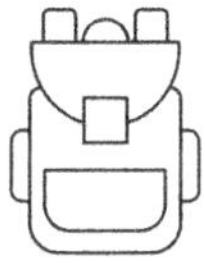

Visualize wearing a backpack. If you filled it with all of your sin, would it be heavy? That represents your debt with God. It stops you from having a relationship with Him.

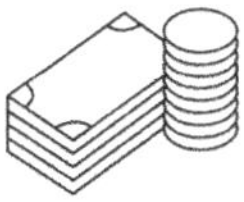

If you owed the bank a million dollars and I gave you a check for that amount, what would happen to your debt if you gave it to the bank?

That's what Jesus did when He died on the cross. He wrote you a check signed in His blood with your name on it. He rose again, and today, He's standing at the door of your heart, wanting you to cash it.

If Jesus were here right now, would you let Him in?

Can you see the wind? No, but you can feel it, right? Like the wind, Jesus is here right now. Can I pray for you to feel His pre ence? (After prayer) What did you feel?

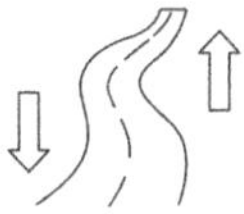

Right now, you're on a road of life without Jesus.
You need to turn from your sin, change direction, and follow Him.
Do you want to follow Him?

Prayer: Jesus, forgive me for my sins. I open the door of my heart. I make You Lord of my life. Fill me with Your spirit. Amen.

Thoughts About Jesus at the Door

- Scott McNamara says, "There is nothing fancy about this method. It simply puts forth the Gospel plain and simple. I felt the Lord highlight 1 Corinthians 2:13 as a passage that best defines what Jesus at the Door really is: 'When we tell you these things, we do not use words that come from human wisdom. Instead, we speak words given to us by the Spirit, using the Spirit's words to explain spiritual truths[30].'"

- The picture of Jesus at the Door comes from the classic painting by the English painter Holman Hunt titled *Jesus the Light of the World.* It is a visual depiction of Revelation 3:20.

- Revelation 3:20 is a picture of Jesus standing outside the door of the church at Laodicea and waiting to be admitted. Jesus does not force Himself on anyone. He patiently waits to be invited in. We also see this in Luke 24:28-32 where Jesus is walking with two of His disciples to Emmaus. When they reached their house in Emmaus, Jesus acted like He would walk further without them. Instead, they invited Jesus to come in. Jesus waited until He was invited to enter their home. This shows that permission is important. God does not force Himself upon anyone. He waits for the door to be opened.

- Scott McNamara perfected this script after hundreds of hours spent witnessing on the street. It is tried and tested.

30 Scott McNamara, *Jesus at the Door*, (Chosen, Bloomington, Minnesota 2020), 17.

CHAPTER 17

HONOR RESTORED

Key Scriptures: Genesis 1:1, 27, 31; Psalm 8:1,5; Romans 1:1, 3:23, 6:23; Isaiah 59:2, Isaiah, 53:3,4; Hebrews 12:2; Romans 4:25; Romans 10:9,11; John 1:12

Honor Restored Script

Source: This script can be found on Cru's GodTools[31] app. Many of the concepts found behind the Honor Restored method of presenting the Gospel have been developed by Jayson Georges on the Honorshame.com website.

WHAT TO SAY:

Can I share with you what the Bible says about our longing to be included or accepted?

What is shame? Shame is when we feel isolated, rejected, polluted, excluded, and abandoned. (*In this picture, the bowed head and the crooked line above the head represent the shame a person feels when they do something shameful.*)

Can our shame be removed?

What is honor? Honor is when we are included, accepted, exalted, cleansed, and cherished. (*The upright head with the lines of glory surrounding it represent a person who is standing tall because he or she has received great honor.*)

31 https://godtoolsapp.com/en/

Can our honor be restored?

1. **The Beginning:** God created a good world and gave humanity great dignity.

The good world reflected God's love and greatness.

"In the beginning, God created the heavens and the earth…So God created human beings in his own likeness. He created them to be like himself…. God saw everything he had made. And it was very good" (Genesis 1:1, 27, 31).

Under God's care, people honored Him rightly as their Father and lived in perfect relationships. *"Lord, our Lord, how majestic is your name in the whole earth. You have set your glory in the heavens... You have made [humanity] a little lower than the angels. You placed on them a crown of glory and honor"* (Psalm 8:1,5).

If God created a good world, why does it feel so broken?

2. **The Problem:** We rebelled against our Creator. We sought glory apart from God and dishonored Him.

The first man and woman, Adam and Eve, disobeyed God, and this sin brought shame upon the entire human race.

By cutting ourselves off from the source of true honor and life, we corrupted the world and brought death, the ultimate state of shame.

"They knew God. But they didn't honor him as God...Everyone has sinned. No one measures up to God's glory.... When you sin, the pay you get is death" (Romans 1:1, 3:23, 6:23).

For example, think about the shame someone might feel if they are caught stealing something that does not belong to them.

We feel shame because we have dishonored God and our relationship with Him is broken.

"But your iniquities (sins) have separated you from your God; your sins have hidden His face from you, so that He will not hear." (Isaiah 59:2 NIV).

Can we solve this problem of shame?

3. The Solution: God loves us so much that He sent Jesus to restore us from brokenness.

Jesus lived an honorable life and suffered a shameful death. Though Jesus lived a perfect life, He was mocked, rejected, and abandoned. He suffered an unjust and shameful death on a cross.

"We looked down on Him. We didn't have any respect for Him. He suffered the things we should have suffered. He took on Himself the pain that should have been ours." (Isaiah, 53:3,4).

Often people ask, "Why did Jesus suffer such a shameful death?" The answer is that Jesus took our shame upon Himself so that we can be set free from shame. (*Notice the crooked line of shame is now on Jesus' head as a crown of thorns. This shows how Jesus took our shame upon Himself at the cross. Jesus was shamed so that we do not have to suffer from shame any longer.*)

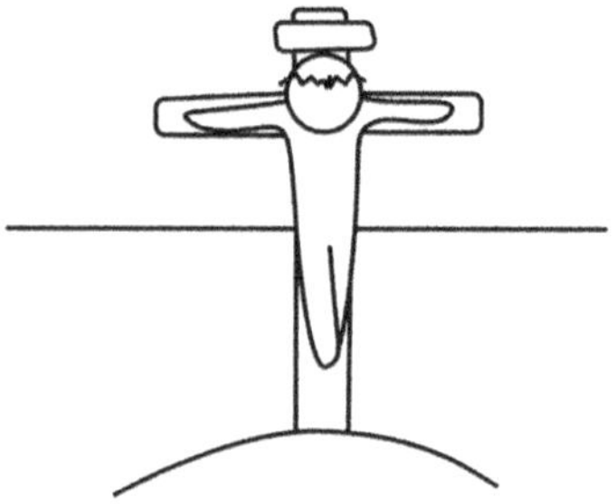

Jesus removed our guilt and shame. He gladly took our sin, removing our guilt and absorbing our shame.

"Because of the joy awaiting Him, [Jesus] endured the cross, disregarding its shame. Now He is seated at the place of honor beside God's throne" (Hebrews 12:2b).

Jesus rose from the dead vindicated and honored by God. Only He can reconcile us to God.

"Jesus was handed over to die for our sins. He was raised to life in order to make us right with God" (Romans 4:25).

4. Our Response: We must turn away from seeking our own honor and trust God.

We must embrace Jesus with complete loyalty and trust.

"Say with your mouth, 'Jesus is Lord." Believe in your heart that God raised Him from the dead. Then you will be saved... The one who believes in Him will never be put to shame" (Romans 10:9,11).

In order to receive God's honor, we must allow God to be our source of honor as His beloved children.

"Some people did accept Him and did believe in His name. He gave them the right to become children of God" (John 1:12).

Now, you face a choice. Do you want to trust Jesus to bear your shame and receive His honor? Why or why not?

If you want God to remove your shame and give you honor, you can express your desire through a simple prayer.

Heavenly Father, I am in need of You. I confess that I have sought honor apart from You. As a result, I have dishonored You, and my heart is impure. I thank You that Jesus willingly entered into my shame, took it upon Himself, and now invites me to share in His honor. I believe in Jesus alone for honor and adoption into Your family. I desire to follow You with my whole being. Make me the person that You want me to be. Amen.

Thoughts About Honor Restored

- Throughout the West, most Gospel presentations use personal guilt to demonstrate a need for a Savior. We focus on ideas like, "I am a sinner. I have done wrong. I need forgiveness."

This is because Western society is a guilt-based society.

However, many of the world's cultures place a higher emphasis on shame and honor. This happens frequently in the East where "saving face" is a top priority. In these cultures, saving one's honor can be a higher value than guilt or innocence. For example, I read a news story from Pakistan where three brothers killed their sister because she went outside the house in skimpy clothing. The brothers felt that her state of undress brought extreme dishonor and shame upon their family, and it was better for her to die than for the family's honor to be questioned. In other words, restoring the family's honor was more important to her brothers than the guilt that they would endure for murdering her.

Honor and shame cultures are based on different principles and values than guilt-based cultures. In a shame culture, one's social standing is based on how they are perceived by others, and a person's reputation is considered vital. Shame is a negative emotion felt when a person violates cultural expectations or norms, and it can come from family, community, or society as a whole. On the other hand, honor is a positive value that a person earns by upholding cultural norms, and is publicly recognized. Honor can be lost through actions that bring shame and dishonor to the individual or their family. In a shame culture, honor can be restored through public demonstrations of remorse and reparations to regain one's standing in the community.

In these cultures where there is a deep understanding of shame and honor, the Honor Restored Gospel presentation can be more effective than a guilt-based presentation.

In Western cultures, we often do not understand the reality of shame, but the Bible actually has a lot to say about honor and shame. Western presentations of the Gospel often include Romans

10:9-10, but they rarely include the very next verse. Romans 10:11 says, "As Scripture says, *"Anyone who believes in him will never be put to shame."*

When ministering in honor/shame-based cultures, it is helpful to present the Gospel using terms that are meaningful in that culture.

*Here is an outline of the Gospel of Salvation for an Honor/Shame Society from Jayson Georges:[32]

The Problem: Unfaithfulness
People have broken their relationship with God. Our sin dishonors God. (Ez 36:21; Romans 1:21-23. 2:23, 3:23)

The Dilemma: Shame
Our dishonor means separation and disunion. We are shameful in God's eyes and feel shame. (Gen 3:7-8; Jeremiah 3:8, 25; Romans 1:24)

The Solution: Restoration
Jesus' death honored God and bore our shame. His death reconciled the relationship. (Isaiah 50:6; Hebrews 12:2; Romans 8:14f).

Our Response: Loyalty
People must honor Jesus with complete allegiance. We must seek God's face and name. (1 Samuel 2:30; John 12:26, 43; Romans 4:20f).

The Result: Honor
God makes outcasts His children and exalts them to eternal glory. (Zeph 3:19; Isa 54:4; 62:2f; John 1:12; 17:22; Romans 10:11-12; 1 Peter 2:6-11).

32 Jayson Georges, "The Gospel in Five Words," (Accessed February 10, 2023) https://honorshame.com/the-gospel-in-5-words/

CHAPTER 18

THE CRADLE, THE CROSS, AND THE CROWN

Key Scriptures: Luke 2:11-12, 1 Corinthians 15:3-4, Acts 2:21

Source: Daniel King

The Cradle, the Cross, and the Crown

There is born to you this day in the city of David a Savior, who is Christ the Lord. And this will be the sign to you: You will find a Babe wrapped in swaddling cloths, lying in a manger" (Luke 2:11-12)

Christ died for our sins according to the Scriptures, and He was buried, and He rose again the third day. (1 Corinthians 15:3-4)

Whoever calls on the name of Jesus shall be saved. (Acts 2:21)

WHAT TO SAY:

From the Cradle…

Two thousand years ago, a tiny baby was born in the city of Bethlehem. He was born in a stable amongst the animals, and He was laid in a manger. His earthly father was a poor carpenter named Joseph, and His mother was a virgin girl named Mary. The baby's real Father was God Himself. Mary named the child Jesus. But the baby had another name. He was also called Immanuel, which means, "God with us." That baby was the King of Kings. He was God Incarnate, the Creator of the entire universe. Yet, He humbled Himself and became a man. The baby deserved global fanfare, but only some shepherds came to see Him.

God became a man because He wanted to save people from their sins. The first man and woman, Adam and Eve, sinned, and this sin separated people from God. God's Book says, "All have sinned and fallen short of the glory of God." Sin is when we disobey God's commands. Lying, stealing, and hating your brother are examples of sin. Every single person has done something wrong. We have all sinned. Sin separates us from God.

Over the centuries, people have tried many different ways to get reconnected with God, but none of them were successful. Some people thought money would buy them a place in heaven, but no amount of money is enough. Others formulated religious rituals in an effort to get to God, but the rituals were useless. Others thought that they could find a way to God if they became smart enough, but their study was wasted. Since it was impossible for people to get to God, God decided to become a human being and come to us. Jesus was born in order to provide a way for us to have a relationship with God.

…To the Cross…

God's book says, "The price for sin is death, but the gift of God is eternal life through Jesus Christ."

Because of our sins, we deserve to die and to be eternally separated from God. However, God does not want us to separate from Him, so He sent His only Son Jesus Christ to be born here on earth. The Bible says, "For God so loved the world that He gave His only begotten Son, that whoever believes in Him should not perish but have everlasting life."

Jesus never sinned. He lived a perfect life. He did not deserve to die, but He gave up His life to provide a way for people to be saved. Jesus stretched out His hands and He was nailed to a cross. His death paid the price for your sin. The cross that Jesus died on is the bridge between heaven and earth. He died so that we can live.

...To the Crown!

However, Jesus did not stay dead. After three days, Jesus rose from the dead! Today, Jesus is alive. He is sitting in heaven with a crown on His head. He is now the King of the Universe, and He wants to be the King of your heart.

The Bible promises, "Everyone who calls on the Name of the Lord shall be saved." If you will cry out to Jesus today, He will save you from your sin and you will be perfect and holy before God. The Bible promises, "if you confess with your mouth the Lord Jesus and believe in your heart that God has raised Him from the dead, you will be saved."

If you want Jesus to forgive your sins, I encourage you to pray this prayer: "Dear God in Heaven, I believe Jesus died on the cross. I believe Jesus rose from the dead. Today, I choose to make Jesus the Lord of my life. I repent of all of my sin. Please forgive me. In Jesus' Name, Amen."

Thoughts About The Cradle, the Cross, and the Crown

- This is a powerful illustration to use at Christmas time. Christmas time is a great time to talk to people about God. They are thinking about Christmas and giving gifts, and their hearts are open to receive. The Cradle, the Cross, and the Crown is a great outline to talk to people about Jesus, the Reason for the Season.

- Recently, I was asked by Terry Henshaw from CityServeOK to lead evangelism teams for a Christmas outreach here in Tulsa, Oklahoma every night from December 1-18. Their ministry transformed the entire second story of the Promenade Mall into a Christmas Wonderland. It was full of Christmas lights and décor along with music and experiences for the family. In Santa's workshop, children assembled a wooden yo-yo to take home. In another room was a Christmas Tree maze ending with Elsa, Anna, and Olaf characters. There was a petting zoo, a reindeer barn, and a huge room of model trains. The kids met Santa and Mrs. Claus and ate a Christmas cookie with hot chocolate.

The most important room in the whole place was the living Nativity scene where guests viewed a live enactment of the birth of Jesus. As families passed the living Nativity, shepherds beckoned them into the ministry room where we had the opportunity to pray with them and make sure that they are going to heaven.

As families entered, the children were invited to sit and were given a coloring sheet with pictures of a cradle, a cross, and a crown. As the kids colored, we used those three elements to tell the entire family about the real story of Christmas.

Every night a different local church volunteered to pray for people.

Each evening I taught a new group of believers how to share their faith using The Cradle, the Cross, and the Crown illustration. This was an exciting opportunity for me because an important part of my calling as an evangelist is to encourage and train believers to share their faith with the lost.

The numbers communicate the impact of this outreach: 18 Days! 72 hours of ministry! Over 250 people trained in evangelism! 4,188 interactions and prayers for people! 733 people prayed with us for salvation! 23 healed!

CHAPTER 19

THE APPLE WITNESSING STICKER

The Apple Witnessing Sticker

When Steve Jobs (founder of the Apple computer company) designed his logo, he deliberately chose to use the icon of an apple with a bite taken out of it. He chose this logo because it represented "forbidden knowledge." This is a clear reference to the "fruit" that Adam and Eve ate in the Garden of Eden in disobedience to God's command to stay away from the "tree of the knowledge of good and evil." Since Steve Jobs used an apple with a bite, I figured I might as well use the apple as a witnessing tool.

Ever since I put this Apple Witnessing Sticker on the back of my laptop, people in coffee shops ask me questions about it. Each time, I take the opportunity to share the Gospel. I have led several people to Jesus because of this sticker. When you put this sticker on the back of your Apple computer, God will turn your Apple computer into a tool for sharing the Gospel.

How to Witness Using the Apple Witnessing Sticker

The Gospel can be shared with four simple truths:

God's Creation: *Point to the tree.* At the beginning of time, God created the whole universe. Everything God created has a purpose. The birds were made to fly, the fish were made to swim, the trees were made to give us fruit, and God created Adam and Eve to be His friends. (Key Verse: Genesis 1:1)

Satan's Deception: *Point to Adam and Eve.* One day, Satan came and tempted Adam and Eve with a fruit. In fact, some people think that Steve Jobs chose the apple with a bite out of it to represent "forbidden knowledge." Adam and Eve disobeyed God by eating the forbidden fruit and this sin separated them from God. Anytime we disobey God, our disobedience is called sin. The Bible says, "all have sinned and fallen short of the glory of God." (Key Verse: Romans 3:23).

Christ's Substitution: *Point to the Cross.* The Bible says that "the price for sin is death." But God loves us so much that He sent His only Son, Jesus Christ, from heaven to earth to pay the price for our sins. The Bible says, "The Gift of God is eternal life through Jesus Christ…" Jesus loves you so much that He stretched out His arms and gave His life on a wooden cross. (Key Verses: John 3:16, Romans 6:23).

Our Salvation: *Point to Adam and Eve again.* Every person faces a choice. Do you choose to follow a way of sin (*point to the apple*), or do you choose to trust Jesus to forgive your sins (*point to the crosses*)? The Bible says, "Everyone who calls on the name of the Lord shall be saved." If you will call on Jesus, He will save you from your sins and give you a wonderful relationship with God. (Key verse: Acts 2:21).

To order a copy of the Apple Witnessing Sticker, please visit: www.kingministries.com

Final Note: The Doctrine of Fair Use

Copyright laws exist to protect the intellectual property rights of creators and owners of original works. However, recognizing the importance of free expression and the advancement of knowledge, copyright laws also include provisions for fair use. Fair use is a legal doctrine that allows for the limited use of copyrighted material for specific purposes, such as non-profit, educational, scholarly use, criticism, and commentary, without obtaining permission from the owner.

The purpose behind fair use is to balance the interests of creators, owners, and users by promoting the dissemination of knowledge and encouraging creative expression. For example, in an educational context, the use of copyrighted material in a classroom lecture, or the inclusion of a portion of a copyrighted work in a scholarly paper, is often considered fair use. Similarly, criticism and commentary often involve the use of copyrighted material as a means of making a point or demonstrating the relevance of an issue.

Fair use provisions in copyright laws are important for allowing for the free exchange of ideas and the advancement of knowledge, while still protecting the rights of creators and owners. By providing a balance between the interests of various stakeholders, fair use helps to foster creativity and critical thinking and encourages the free flow of information and ideas.

There have been many different methods that are used for communicating the Gospel. Each method seeks to communicate truth using illustrations and stories. The copyright to these methods is automatically owned by the person or organization who first develops the material.

In this book, I have tried to find the balance between following the law with respect to copyright and the fair use of these witnessing methods:

1. This book is published by a non-profit organization, and it will be used exclusively for non-profit purposes. The book is also educational in nature. It exists in order to educate people in various methods of sharing the Gospel.

2. I have attempted to give credit for each witnessing method including links to websites where people can access the original method. Over the years, some of these methods have been used, reused, and reinterpreted, so at times, it is impossible to tell who owns the original copyright. Regardless, I have done my best to track down each method of witnessing to its origin and to give credit where credit is due.

3. It is necessary to explain in detail how each method of witnessing works which is why I have included so much material from so many different methods of witnessing. I have added my commentary and, at times, my criticism of each method. Since I am adding original research and ideas, it makes the use of this material "fair use."

3. The purpose of this book is to help people become better at sharing the Gospel. I hope and pray that every ministry and believer who wants people to be saved would be willing to broadly share their methods that can be used to bring people to Jesus. When it comes to Christian attitudes toward copyright laws, I like T.L. Osborn's approach. He said, "If you copy my teaching, please make sure you copy it right." In other words, we should consider copyright more from a kingdom mindset instead of from a secular mindset.

About the Author

Dr. Daniel King is a missionary evangelist who has traveled to over seventy nations in his quest for souls. His goal is to lead 1,000,000 people to Jesus every year through massive Gospel Festivals, distribution of literature, and leadership training.

Because of his experience and research on evangelism, he is widely regarded as one of the world's leading experts in mass evangelism. He has spoken to more than 2,000 live audiences around the world with attendance of up to 50,000 people and has led over two million individuals in a salvation prayer.

Daniel is the host of *The Evangelism Podcast*, a popular program known for sharing powerful stories about what God is doing around the world, for training evangelists and everyday believers to share their faith, and for exploring the best methods for church growth. He is often called "The Evangelism Coach" because of his passion for training other evangelists.

Daniel graduated *summa cum laude* from Oral Roberts University in 2002 with a B.A. degree in New Testament Studies, with a Master of Divinity degree in 2014, and with a Doctorate of Ministry degree in 2019. The focus of his doctoral research was mass evangelism.

He was called into the ministry when he was five years old and began to preach when he was six. His parents became missionaries to Mexico when he was ten. Daniel spent the next thirteen years ministering in Mexico alongside his parents. When he was fourteen he started a children's ministry that gave him the opportunity to minister in some of America's largest churches while he was still a teenager. Daniel recently celebrated twenty years of full-time ministry.

He is the author of over twenty books including *The Secret of Obed-Edom, Healing Power, Fire Power, Soul Winning,* and *Grace Wins.* Over 600,000 of his books are in print.

He is married to Jessica. They have two children, Caleb and Katie Grace and they live in Tulsa, Oklahoma, USA.

Daniel is available to speak at your church or conference on apologetics or evangelism.

To invite him to your event or for evangelism coaching, please visit:

www.KingMinistries.com

Gospel Festivals Around the World

Abuna, Ethiopia

Kemba, Ethiopia

Chuko, Ethiopia

Agara Marium
Ethiopia

Metu, Ethiopia

Lalo Kile, Ethiopia

Ambo, Ethiopia

Wondo Genet, Ethiopia

Kihihi, Uganda

Diego, Madagascar

Antananarivo, Madagascar

Sambava, Madagascar

Nosy-Be, Madagascar

Cape Haitian,
Haiti

Kwade Bouke,
Haiti

Ouanaminthe,
Haiti

Montego Bay,
Jamaica

Holguin,
Cuba

Azua, DR

Puerto Plata, DR

Barahona, Dominican Republic

Cartagena, Colombia

Sobral, Brazil

Iquitos, Peru

Jequié, Brazil

Caicó, Brazil

Crato, Brazil

Brasília, Brazil

Belo Horizonte, Brazil

Your Support Makes Miracles Happen!

God is Moving Around the World!

Escuintla,
Guatemala

Copan, Honduras

Intibuca,
Honduras

Belize City, Belize

Palma Sur,
Costa Rica

Roca Blanca, Mexico

GRAN CAMPAÑA
DE MILAGROS
Juarez, Mexico

La Chorrera, Panama

Hear the Testimonies
Experience the Miracles
Watch the Videos

The vision of King Ministries

is to lead 1,000,000 people to Jesus every year

and to train believers to become leaders.

To contact Daniel & Jessica King:

Write:

King Ministries International

PO Box 701113

Tulsa, OK 74170 USA

King Ministries Canada

PO Box 3401

Morinville, Alberta T8R 1S3 Canada

Call toll-free:

1-877-431-4276

Visit us online:

www.KingMinistries.com

E-Mail:

daniel@kingministries.com

Made in the USA
Middletown, DE
03 May 2025

75063448R00106